Simple, flavorful recipes that make healthy eating easy, even on your busiest days.

From quick weeknight dinners to nourishing meals that don't sacrifice flavor, Jazz Leaf brings you a collection of recipes designed to fit seamlessly into your life. With her approachable style and focus on simplicity, this cookbook is packed with dishes you can make in 30 minutes or less, using 10 ingredients or fewer. Whether you're a seasoned cook or just starting out, Jazz's recipes will help you create healthy, satisfying meals without the stress.

Drawing from her experience as a private chef for professional athletes and her own journey as a busy mom and business owner, Jazz knows what it takes to balance great food with a hectic schedule. Inside, you'll find everything from vibrant salads and hearty mains to indulgent yet better-for-you desserts. Each recipe is crafted to make cooking fun, achievable, and delicious. With Jazz as your guide, you'll discover how simple it can be to nourish yourself and your family with meals you'll truly enjoy.

jazz leaf

table of contents

About Me

Breakfast

Smoothies

Appetizers & Sides

Salads

Pasta & Pizza

Vegetarian

table of contents

Chicken, Beef & Turkey

Fish & Seafood

Dressings & Sauces

Snacks and Dessert

How To Shop

COOKBOOK / COOKBOOK / COOKBOOK /

"Let thy food be
thy medicine
and medicine
be thy food"

Hippocrates

about

Hi, I'm Jazz! I'm a wife, mom to my sweet daughter Olive, and a business owner passionate about helping people simplify life and eat well. But it wasn't always this way—my journey to where I am now has been anything but a straight line.

After graduating from UC Santa Barbara, I dove headfirst into the corporate world as a project manager. On paper, it looked like I had it all figured out, but deep down, I knew something was missing. I craved purpose and connection, especially through food—a love I'd always had but never pursued seriously. So, I decided to shake things up and enrolled in Nutritional Therapy. That one bold step opened a door to an entirely new world.

In 2017, I took another leap of faith and moved to Indianapolis, determined to work in the food industry. My dream? To fuel others—literally. I became a private chef for some of the Indiana Pacers, spending my days creating elaborate meals designed to keep them at the top of their game. But here's the irony: after long hours in the kitchen, I'd come home exhausted, with only enough energy to slap together a PB&J or pour a bowl of cereal. It was clear something wasn't adding up. How could I help others eat so well while my own meals felt like an afterthought?

Then, in 2019, life handed me a hard reset. While biking to the beach, I was hit by a car—a moment that turned my world upside down. It was a wake-up call that reminded me how fragile life is and how important it is to focus on what truly matters: living intentionally, nourishing my body, and helping others do the same.

That moment became my turning point. I realized my purpose wasn't just about fancy meals for athletes but about helping everyday people—busy moms, overwhelmed beginners, anyone who felt stuck in the kitchen—create simple, healthy, and realistic meals without the stress.

Now, I'm here to share everything I've learned, from my time in corporate to professional kitchens, to navigating the ups and downs of life. My mission is to make cooking approachable, fun, and something you actually look forward to. Whether you're short on time, feeling lost in the kitchen, or just looking to nourish yourself and your loved ones better, I've got you. Together, we'll turn cooking into something simple, satisfying, and totally doable. Let's make mealtime the easiest—and most rewarding—part of your day!

breakfast

The most important meal, simplified

A healthy breakfast is more than just a morning routine, it's the foundation of your day. Starting your day with a balanced meal helps stabilize your blood sugar, fuels your energy levels, and supports focus and mood throughout the day. That's why the recipes in this section are designed to be simple, nutritious, and beginner-friendly. From high-protein options to fiber-packed choices, these breakfasts will keep you satisfied and ready to tackle whatever comes your way. Let's make healthy eating easy, one morning at a time!

TACO BELL BREAKFAST CRUNCHWRAP

Yield: 1 | Total Time: 25 Min

I make this for my husband for breakfast when we are celebrating one of his accomplishments, it marries his love for a breakfast burrito and a quesadilla into one!

INGREDIENTS

- 2 tortillas, 1 large and 1 small
- 1 frozen hash brown
- 2 strips of bacon
- 2 eggs, whisked
- 1/4 teaspoon salt
- 1/8 teaspoon black pepper
- 1 teaspoon butter
- 1/2 cup shredded cheddar cheese
- 1 avocado spread pouch
- Avocado oil cooking spray
- Chile lime crema (see page 183)

INSTRUCTIONS

1. Place the frozen hash brown into one side of your air fryer. Air fry at 400F for 14 minutes until golden and crispy.

2. Line the other side of the air fryer basket with foil. Place the bacon into the air fryer on top of the foil in a single layer. Air fry at 350F for 11 minutes.

3. Crack your eggs into a small bowl. Add the 1/4 teaspoon of salt and the 1/8 teaspoon of pepper. Whisk until foamy.

4. Heat a skillet on the stove on low heat. Add your butter and allow it to melt. Next add your eggs and allow them to cook slowly. Stir them occasionally for about 3 minutes until they are set.

5. In a small bowl, stir together Greek yogurt, lime juice and chili powder. Mix until smooth.

6. Spray your air fryer basket with non-stick cooking spray to prep.

7. Place the large tortilla on a cutting board. To the center of the tortilla, add the bacon, scrambled eggs, chile lime crema, hash brown, and avocado spread.

8. Finish with a small tortilla in the center.

9. Fold the edges of the tortilla around the smaller tortilla pleating until fully closed.

10. Place the crunchwrap seam-side down in the air fryer so it does not open up. Spray the top with a coat of the non-stick spray.

11. Air fry at 380F for 8 minutes, flipping halfway through.

12. Once finished, both sides will be golden brown.

13. Lay it on the cutting board for a few minutes, then cut in half to serve!

EASY AIR FRYER BAGELS

Yield: 4 Bagels | Total Time: 15 Min

I never buy bagels anymore. I always just make my own with this easy 15-minute recipe. They taste better than store-bought bagged bagels, and I love how much protein they have in them!

INGREDIENTS

- 1 cup whole milk plain Greek yogurt, strained (make sure the yogurt is really thick)
- 1 cup flour or gluten-free flour
- 1 1/2 teaspoons baking powder
- 1/2 teaspoon salt
- Avocado oil spray
- Everything bagel seasoning (optional topping)

INSTRUCTIONS

1. Combine the flour, baking powder and salt into a big bowl. I like to run it through a sieve to remove all of the clumps.

2. Add the yogurt to the flour mixture, use a spatula to mix the dough until it comes together. Alternatively, you can use your hands to bring the dough together. Sometimes, it's easier that way! I like to put on gloves & get messy right there on the kitchen counter.

3. At this point, you may need to add a bit more flour or yogurt until you reach the desired dough consistency. It should NOT stick to your hands. If it sticks to your fingers, add more flour. If it is too crumbly and doesn't form into a ball, just add more yogurt (about 1 teaspoon at a time).

4. Divide the dough into 4 equal parts, roll out each part with your hands to form a small rope. Put the ends together to make a round circle (bagel shape).

5. Spray your air fryer with avocado oil spray, then place your bagels in the air fryer. Spray the top of the bagel. Sprinkle with your favorite seasoning (everything bagel seasoning, cheese, sesame seeds, sea salt etc.).

6. Air fry at 400F for about 10 minutes, until golden.

7. Wait for them to cool, then slice them open and add your favorite toppings!

BALSAMIC TOMATO AVOCADO TOAST

Yield: 1 Serving | Total Time: 5 Min

INGREDIENTS

- 2 slices of your favorite bread
- 1 large avocado
- 1 tomato, sliced
- 1 tablespoon balsamic glaze or balsamic vinegar
- 1 teaspoon olive oil
- 1/4 teaspoon sea salt
- 1/8 teaspoon black pepper

INSTRUCTION

1. Toast your bread in the toaster.
2. Mash the avocado on a small plate and spread it evenly on the toasted bread.
3. Arrange your tomato slices on top of the avocado.
4. Drizzle with balsamic glaze, olive oil, salt and pepper to taste.

Jazz's Tricks!

Try this with your favorite bagel.
Add a fried egg on top for protein.
Add a layer of pesto before the avocado for some extra flavor.
Enjoy immediately!

GRAB-AND-GO VEGGIE EGG BITES

Yield:12 Muffins | Total Time: 45 Min

When we are anticipating a busy week, I make a batch of these egg bites for breakfast. We eat them on the go, and my husband loves adding hot sauce on top! It's a great way to get rid of veggies in the fridge!

INGREDIENTS

- 8 large eggs
- 1/4 cup water
- 1 bell pepper, diced
- 1 small red onion, diced
- 2 cups spinach or kale, thinly sliced
- 1 cup shredded cheese
- 1/2 teaspoon salt
- 1/2 teaspoon basil
- 1/2 teaspoon oregano
- 1/4 teaspoon pepper
- Avocado oil spray, butter or olive oil (for not sticking)

INSTRUCTIONS

1. Preheat your oven to 350 degrees Fahrenheit.

3. Whisk together the 8 eggs with ¼ cup water. Add the 1 teaspoon of salt, 1/2 teaspoon basil, 1/2 teaspoon oregano and ¼ teaspoon of pepper into the egg mixture.

4. Use a hand blender or whisk to whisk everything together well.

5. Grease 12 muffin cups with avocado oil, olive oil or butter. If you are using a true non-stick muffin pan, you won't need to grease and you can skip this step.

6. Add about 1 tablespoon of diced onion into each muffin cup, followed by 1 tablespoon of diced bell pepper and 1–2 tablespoons of spinach.

7. Add the whisked egg on top of the veggies, about ⅔ of the way full.

8. Finish with a sprinkle of cheese on each muffin cup. You can add more or less depending on how cheesy you like it.

9. Place the muffins into the oven for 18 minutes.

10. The egg muffins will come out puffy when they are pulled out of the oven, but then deflate a few minutes later. This is totally normal.

11. Let them cool for about 5-10 minutes.

12. Top with optional hot sauce, salsa, or diced avocado.

Storage

- They can be eaten cold or warm (pop in the microwave for 30 seconds)!
- Store in the fridge for up to 4 days.
- Freeze these in between parchment paper for up to 3 months, thaw them in the fridge week by week!

EVERYTHING BAGEL VEGGIE TACOS

Yield: 3 Tacos | Total Time: 18 Min

INGREDIENTS

- 3 tortillas, any kind
- 1/3 cup plain full-fat Greek yogurt, swap for plain non-dairy yogurt
- 1/3 cup canned chickpeas, drained and rinsed
- 1/4 cup red onion, sliced
- 1/4 cup bell pepper, sliced
- 1/2 avocado, sliced
- 2 handfuls of spinach, swap for kale
- 1 tablespoon lemon juice
- 2 teaspoons olive oil
- 1 teaspoon Everything But the Bagel seasoning
- 1/2 teaspoon salt
- 1/2 teaspoon turmeric
- 1/4 teaspoon pepper

INSTRUCTIONS

1. Heat the tortillas in a non-stick skillet on the stove on medium-high heat for about 45 seconds on each side. Once heated, remove and set aside.

2. In the same heated pan, add avocado oil, red onion, chickpeas, and bell pepper. Cook for about 5 minutes, stirring throughout to cook evenly.

3. Remove from the heat, then add the spinach and lemon juice. Allow the spinach to wilt in the warm pan.

4. Smear a layer of plain Greek yogurt evenly on each warm tortilla.

5. Add the warm veggie filling evenly on top of the Greek yogurt.

6. Add the sliced avocado to the top.

7. Sprinkle each with everything bagel seasoning.

8. Enjoy!

OVERNIGHT VEGAN & PALEO CHIA PUDDING RECIPE

Yield: 3 Jars of Chia Seed Pudding | Total Time: 2 H & 10 M

I have to say, this is my favorite breakfast to meal prep. I could have this every single day, 365 days a year. It's paleo, high-protein, high-fiber and such a great way to start the day!

INGREDIENTS

- 1 can (12 oz) unsweetened coconut milk
- 1/2 cup any plant-based milk
- 1/2 cup chia seeds
- 1 teaspoon vanilla extract
- 2 tablespoons - 1/4 cup maple syrup, depending on preference (swap for honey or agave)
- 1/2 teaspoon cinnamon
- 1/4 teaspoon salt
- Optional: 1-2 scoops of collagen or protein powder

Optional Toppings

- Fresh berries
- Banana slices
- Homemade granola (see page 22)
- Cacao nibs or chocolate chips
- Coconut flakes

INSTRUCTIONS

1. Mix everything in a large bowl and whisk. Continue whisking every minute until the chia seeds begin to thicken. They will continue to thicken in the fridge. This process helps remove any clumps.

2. Pour mixture evenly into 3 glass jars with lids, refrigerate for at least 6 hours or overnight! This lasts about 4 days in the fridge!

3. Top with your favorite toppings just before eating.

CHOCOLATE PROTEIN SMOOTHIE BOWL (NO BANANA)

Yield:1 Serving | Total Time: 5 Min

INGREDIENTS

Smoothie Base

- 1 cup frozen zucchini slices
- 3/4 cup frozen cauliflower florets
- 1/4 cup frozen avocado slices
- 2 Medjool dates, pitted
- 2 tablespoons chia seeds, hemp seeds or flax seeds
- 1 serving of chocolate protein powder or collagen
- 2 tablespoons cacao powder
- 1 cup liquid of choice (i.e. coconut milk, almond milk, coconut water)

There are so many benefits of this banana free smoothie bowl! It's low in sugar, vegan, gluten-free, high-protein and delicious!

Optional Toppings

- 1/4 cup homemade granola - use my granola recipe (see page 22)
- 1/4 cup fresh blueberries, raspberries or strawberries
- 2 tablespoons coconut flakes
- 1 tablespoon cacao nibs or chocolate chips
- 1-2 tablespoons nut or seed butter

INSTRUCTIONS

1. Add all of the smoothie base ingredients to a high-powered blender (I prefer using one with a tamper).

2. Begin on low speed and add additional liquid as needed (about 2 tablespoons at a time).

3. Use the tamper to move the smoothie contents around until combined.

4. Slowly increase the speed on the blender as you continue to move the tamper.

5. Patiently allow the blender to blend the smoothie until smooth.

6. Transfer the smoothie into a bowl and top with your favorite toppings. Enjoy immediately!

Jazz's Tricks!

Add more or less liquid depending on how thick or thin you want your smoothie! The more liquid you add, the more of a smoothie consistency you will get. The less liquid you add, the more creamy and thick the consistency will be!

EASY VEGAN BLENDER PROTEIN WAFFLES

Yield: 3 Waffles | Total time: 30 Min

This is the only waffle recipe that comes out perfect every time. Whenever I have too many ripe bananas, I make a big batch of these and freeze the rest! It's perfect for kids!

INGREDIENTS

Waffles

- 2 cups oats
- 2 medium bananas, the riper the better
- 1 1/2 cups milk of choice
- 1 scoop of protein powder
- 1/2 teaspoon baking powder
- 1/2 teaspoon apple cider vinegar

Toppings (optional)

- Chocolate chips
- Fresh blueberries
- Coconut whipped cream
- Maple syrup
- Peanut butter

INSTRUCTIONS

1. Add the 2 cups of oats into a high-powered blender and pulse for 20 seconds until oat flour is formed. This doesn't have to be a super fine flour.

2. Into the oats, add 1/2 teaspoon baking powder and 1 scoop of protein powder of choice. Blend again for 10 seconds.

3. Add the 2 ripe bananas, 1 1/2 cups milk of choice and apple cider vinegar. Blend again on low for 20-30 seconds until the batter is smooth.

4. Let the batter sit in the fridge for 5-10 minutes while you prep the toppings and waffle iron.

5. Spray your waffle iron with avocado oil spray. Allow it to heat up completely, then add some of the batter to the waffle iron.

6. Wait until the light turns green and the waffles are cooked. Remove the cooked waffle and repeat until all of the batter is used up and the waffles are formed.

Jazz's Tricks!

Use any flavor protein powder you have. I have tried collagen (unflavored), vanilla, chocolate and peanut butter. All of them turn out amazing!

THE EASIEST HOMEMADE GRANOLA

Yield: 8 Cups | Total Time: 30 Min

I have not bought store-bought granola in years!! This is the only granola recipe I eat. I will often make a big batch over the holidays and gift it to people all around me. Everyone loves it!

INGREDIENTS

- 3 cups oats, quick-cooking or rolled oats work best
- 1 cup nuts or seeds, use any combination
- 1/3 cup maple syrup or any liquid sweetener like honey, agave etc.
- 1/3 cup coconut oil, melted (swap for olive oil)
- 2 teaspoons cinnamon
- 1/2 teaspoon salt

INSTRUCTIONS

1. Preheat oven to 325 degrees Fahrenheit.
2. Combine the dry ingredients in a bowl, mix to combine.
3. Add the wet ingredients into the dry ingredients. Mix well.
4. Lay mixture on a parchment paper lined baking sheet, press down with the back of the spatula.
5. Bake for 15 minutes. Let it cool for an hour before breaking it apart (that's the trick to get the large clusters).
6. Serve on yogurt, or with milk and fresh fruit!

Jazz's Tricks!

Store the granola in an airtight container in your pantry for up to 4 weeks.

Store granola in the fridge for up to 2 months.

Store granola in the freezer in a Ziploc bag for up to 4 months.

To achieve granola clusters, lay flat on a parchment paper-lined baking sheet and press down with the back of a spatula to get it into an even layer. After baking, let it sit for 1 hour before breaking apart to form clusters!

APPLE PIE OATMEAL

Yield: 1 | Total time: 15 Min

INGREDIENTS

- 1 cup plant-based milk, use more if needed
- 1 apple, diced (reserve a few for topping)
- 1/2 cup unsweetened applesauce
- 1/3 cup quick-cooking oats (use gluten-free if necessary)
- 1 tablespoon pure maple syrup or sweetener of choice
- 1 teaspoon ground cinnamon
- 1/2 teaspoon ground ginger
- 1/4 teaspoon ground nutmeg
- 1/4 teaspoon sea salt

Optional toppings:

- Greek yogurt or coconut yogurt
- Raw pecans
- Diced apple
- Walnuts
- Slivered almonds
- Pumpkin seeds
- Coconut whipped cream (see page 196)

INSTRUCTIONS

1. In a medium-sized pot over medium heat, combine all of the ingredients (reserving a few pieces of apple for topping). Mix with a rubber spatula to combine.

2. Cook over medium heat for about 5-8 minutes until thick and creamy. Continue to stir every 1-2 minutes to ensure it doesn't stick to the bottom. Add more liquid as necessary (about 1/4 cup at a time) if you prefer your oatmeal thinner.

3. Once the mixture thickens, it is ready to serve.

4. Pour into a large bowl, add your preferred toppings, and enjoy!

Jazz's Tricks!

This can be made ahead of time and stored in the fridge in an airtight container. It can be eaten cold or warm. Just add the toppings when you are ready to eat.

Stir in a scoop of your favorite vanilla protein powder into the oatmeal base for added protein.

CHOCOLATE CHIP BLENDER PANCAKES

Yield: 1 Large Pancake | Total time: 15 Min

INGREDIENTS

- 1 cup of rolled oats (use certified gluten-free if necessary)
- 1 banana (preferably very ripe & brown)
- 1/2 cup plant-based milk
- 1 scoop of your favorite protein powder
- 1 tablespoon coconut oil + 1 teaspoon for cooking on skillet
- 1/2 teaspoon cinnamon
- 1/4 teaspoon baking powder
- 1/4 teaspoon vanilla extract
- 1/8 teaspoon salt
- 1/4 cup chocolate chips

Optional toppings:

- maple syrup
- honey
- fresh fruit
- jam
- chocolate chips

INSTRUCTIONS

1. Add the oats to a food processor or blender and pulse for about 20 seconds until a flour consistency is attained. Don't worry about getting it super fine, the larger oat flakes will create a nice texture.

2. Add the remaining pancake ingredients into the oat flour, excluding the chocolate chips. Pulse in 5-second increments until everything is incorporated. Be careful not to overmix!

3. Stir in the chocolate chips with a spatula or spoon.

4. Heat a skillet on the stove over medium-high heat and add 1 teaspoon of coconut oil to coat the bottom of the pan.

5. Once the skillet has preheated, pour some of the pancake batter into the pan. You can make each pancake as small or large as you'd like. Cook the pancakes for about 2-4 minutes per side.

6. Serve warm with your favorite pancake topping!

Jazz's Tricks!

For a sweeter pancake batter, add 1 tablespoon of maple syrup to the batter before cooking.

Cook the pancakes in butter as a coconut oil substitute.

Try topping the pancakes with peanut butter or almond butter instead of maple syrup.

Instead of chocolate chips in the pancakes, try adding blueberries!

Store the pancakes in an airtight container in the fridge for up to 3 days or freeze for up to 2 weeks.

From frozen, defrost and heat on a skillet when you're ready to eat.

PEANUT BUTTER CUP OVERNIGHT OATS

Yield: 1 Serving | Total time: 4 Hrs or overnight

INGREDIENTS

- $^{1}/_{2}$ cup dry oats (use certified gluten-free as necessary)
- 1 $^{1}/_{4}$ cup plant-based milk
- 1 scoop chocolate protein powder
- 1 tablespoon peanut butter
- 1 teaspoon unsweetened cocoa powder
- 1 teaspoon maple syrup (optional)
- $^{1}/_{4}$ teaspoon salt

Toppings

- 1 tablespoon peanut butter
- 1-2 tablespoons shaved chocolate or chocolate chips

INSTRUCTIONS

1. Add oats, protein powder, milk, vanilla, sea salt and $^1/_2$ tablespoon of peanut butter to an airtight container or jar. Stir or shake well to combine until all the protein powder has dissolved and peanut butter has dispersed. Seal the container with a lid and place in the fridge for at least 4 hours or overnight.

2. In the morning, remove from the fridge and pour into a bowl. Either heat or serve cold. Top with chocolate chips and remaining peanut butter.

Jazz's Tricks!

Swap the peanut butter for almond butter.

If you want a lower calorie option, swap the peanut butter for powdered peanut butter.

Additional toppings include walnuts, sliced almonds, bananas or strawberries!

Overnight oats will keep for up to 5 days in the fridge in a sealed airtight container, so you can make a batch of these for every morning in your fridge!

CINNAMON CITRUS FRENCH TOAST

Yield: 2 Servings | Total Time: 20 Min

INGREDIENTS

- 4 slices of brioche bread
- 2 eggs
- 1/2 cup orange juice
- 1 teaspoon vanilla extract
- 1/2 teaspoon ground cinnamon
- 1 tablespoon butter + more for topping
- Maple syrup (optional topping)

INSTRUCTIONS

1. In a shallow dish, whisk together the eggs, orange juice, vanilla extract, and ground cinnamon.
2. Heat a large skillet over medium heat and melt a tablespoon of butter.
3. Dip each slice of brioche bread into the batter, ensuring it is evenly coated on both sides.
4. Once the pan is hot, place the coated bread slices onto the skillet. Cook each slice for 2-3 minutes per side, or until golden brown and crispy. If needed, add more butter for subsequent batches.
5. Once all the French toast slices are cooked, transfer them to a plate.
6. Serve immediately with your favorite toppings such as maple syrup, fresh berries, powdered sugar, or whipped cream.

COCONUT BLUEBERRY CHIA PUDDING

Yield: 4 Servings | Total Time: 10 Min (plus chilling time)

INGREDIENTS

For the Pudding:

- 1 can (14 oz) coconut milk
- 1 cup frozen blueberries
- 1/3 cup chia seeds
- 1 teaspoon vanilla extract
- 1/2 teaspoon cinnamon

For the Toppings:

- 1/4 cup shredded coconut
- 1/4 cup pecans, chopped
- 2 tablespoon cacao nibs
- 1/4 teaspoon cinnamon
- Maple syrup for additional sweetness (optional)

INSTRUCTIONS

1. In a high-speed blender, combine the coconut milk, frozen blueberries, chia seeds, vanilla extract, and cinnamon. Blend on high speed for about 30 seconds until the mixture is smooth.

2. Pour the pudding mixture into 4 separate airtight containers. Place the containers in the fridge to thicken for about 30 minutes or overnight.

3. When you are ready to eat, top each serving with shredded coconut, chopped pecans, cacao nibs, and a dash of cinnamon.

4. For extra sweetness, drizzle with maple syrup if desired.

5. Enjoy the chilled pudding.

Jazz's Tricks!

Store the remaining pudding in the fridge for up to 4 days for a quick and easy breakfast throughout the week.

If you prefer a thicker pudding, let it chill for a bit longer or add an extra tablespoon of chia seeds. Feel free to use fresh blueberries instead of frozen ones. You can also substitute pecans with your favorite nuts.

Smoothies

An easy nutrient-packed snack

I'm obsessed with smoothies! They're the easiest way to pack a ton of nutrients into one quick, delicious snack. All of my smoothies are packed with healthy fats and protein and are lower in sugar, keeping you feeling satisfied and energized for longer. Grab a blender, and let's whip up something that's not just simple and nutritious but also irresistibly delicious.

BLUEBERRY CACAO ZUCCHINI SMOOTHIE WITH PROTEIN

Yield: 1 Serving | Total Time: 5 Min

INGREDIENTS

- 1/2 cup frozen blueberries
- 1/2 frozen banana
- 1/2 cup frozen zucchini slices
- 1/2 cup coconut milk
- 1 scoop vanilla protein
- 1 tablespoon chia seeds
- Large handful of spinach (about 2 cups)
- 1 teaspoon of lemon juice
- 1/2 teaspoon cinnamon

My daughter loves this smoothie, it's a great source of fiber, so it's perfect for kids!

Substitutions

- Swap the blueberries for frozen strawberries or mixed berries.
- I use canned coconut milk (it's much creamier), but you could use dairy milk or another plant-based milk. I think oat milk would work great in this recipe.
- Any vanilla protein powder will work!
- Swap the chia seeds for hemp seeds or flaxseeds!
- I love to store my spinach in the freezer, that way it's always cold and ready for smoothies!
- Lemon juice can be omitted, but I highly recommend it as it tastes really refreshing and gives it a zest.

INSTRUCTIONS

1. Blend everything in a high-powered blender & enjoy!

PROTEIN SNICKERS SMOOTHIE

Yield: 1 Serving | Total Time: 5 Min

I often make this protein Snickers smoothie for my husband when he has a sweet tooth. It tastes like your favorite candy bar, but has all the nutrients of a well-balanced meal.

INGREDIENTS

- 1 frozen banana
- 2 tablespoons peanut butter
- 1 scoop chocolate protein
- 1 cup milk of choice
- 1 cup frozen cauliflower florets
- 2 tablespoons agave or 2 pitted dates
- Pinch of salt
- 1 cup ice

Toppings

- 1 tablespoon peanut butter
- 1-2 tablespoons shaved chocolate or chocolate chips

INSTRUCTIONS

1. Add the banana, peanut butter, protein powder, milk, cauliflower florets, sweetener, salt and ice to a high-speed blender.
2. Blend on medium-high for about 30 seconds - 60 seconds until smooth.
3. Meanwhile, melt your dark chocolate chips in a microwave-safe bowl in 30-60 second intervals until smooth and melted (should take about 60 seconds).
4. Smear the melted chocolate on the insides of the serving cup!
5. Pour your smoothie into the cup. Finish with chopped peanuts!
6. Enjoy immediately!

LEAN GREEN VANILLA PROTEIN SMOOTHIE

Yield: 1 Serving | Total Time: 5 Min

INGREDIENTS

- 1 cup frozen avocado cubes
- 1 cup fresh spinach
- 1 frozen banana
- 2 tablespoons almond butter
- 1 date, pitted
- 1/2 teaspoon vanilla extract or vanilla beans
- 1/4 teaspoon pink salt (don't skip this step)
- 1/2 cup - 1 cup of milk of choice

Optional Toppings

- Granola

This is inspired my my favorite smoothie from a cute smoothie shop in downtown Indianapolis, where I used to live for 3 years. I make it from time to time to remind me of the memories!

INSTRUCTIONS

1. Blend all of the ingredients in a high-speed blender on low, then slowly turn to high power for about 60 seconds until smooth and creamy. Be sure to add more liquid if needed. I prefer to begin with less liquid, then work my way little by little, as I like my smoothies more creamy!
2. Serve with your favorite granola, some shredded coconut and any other smoothie toppings of choice!

ALMOND BUTTER SMOOTHIE

Yield: 1 Serving | Total time: 5 Min

INGREDIENTS

- 1 banana, frozen
- 1 cup plant-based milk
- 2 tablespoons almond butter
- 2 scoops chocolate protein powder
- 2 tablespoons cacao powder
- 2 tablespoons flax seeds
- $^{1}/_{2}$ teaspoon ground cinnamon
- 4-6 ice cubes

INSTRUCTIONS

1. Add everything into a high-speed blender and blend for 1 minute.
2. Serve over ice or as is.

Jazz's Tricks!

The browner or riper the banana, the sweeter it is!

To freeze your bananas, remove the skin then store them in a bag or airtight container or freezer baggie in the freezer.

Use any nut or seed butter on hand. Try swapping the almond butter for peanut butter!

Swap the flax seeds for chia seeds or hemp seeds!

Add a handful of fresh spinach for extra greens (you won't taste a thing)!

TROPICAL GREEN SMOOTHIE

Yield: 1 Serving | Total time: 5 Min

INGREDIENTS

- 1 banana, frozen
- $^1/_2$ cup pineapple chunks, frozen
- $^1/_2$ cup cucumber
- 1-2 large handfuls of fresh spinach
- 1-2 cups coconut water (depending on how thick you like your smoothie)
- 1 date, pitted to remove the seed
- 2 scoops vanilla protein powder or collagen (recommended)
- 2 tablespoons chia seeds
- $^1/_2$ teaspoon ginger root, or ground ginger
- 4-6 ice cubes

INSTRUCTIONS

1. Add everything into a high-speed blender and blend for 1 minute.
2. Serve over ice or as is.

Jazz's Tricks!

Substitute the spinach for any other dark leafy greens, like kale!
Substitute the ground chia seeds for hemp seeds or flax seeds.
Swap the coconut water for any other liquid or juice.

COFFEE LOVERS PROTEIN SHAKE

Yield: 1 Serving | Total time: 5 Min

INGREDIENTS

- 1 cup cold brew coffee (or brewed coffee, chilled)
- 2 scoops vanilla protein powder
- 1 cup ice
- 1 tablespoon peanut butter
- 1/2 cup plant-based milk
- 1 tablespoon maple syrup
- 1/4 cup gluten-free rolled oats
- 1 teaspoon vanilla
- 2 dates, pitted
- 1/4 teaspoon cinnamon
- 2 tablespoons ground flaxseeds

INSTRUCTIONS

1. Add everything into a high-speed blender and blend for 1 minute.
2. Serve over ice or as is.

Jazz's Tricks!

Add a handful of frozen cauliflower florets for added fiber and creamy consistency.

Substitute the flaxseeds for chia seeds or hemp seeds.

Substitute the peanut butter for cashew butter.

STRAWBERRIES & CREAM SMOOTHIE

Yield: 1 Serving | Total time: 5 Min

INGREDIENTS

- 1 cup frozen strawberries
- 2 tablespoons flax seeds
- 1 cup canned unsweetened coconut milk
- 1 date, pitted
- 1 cup plain Greek yogurt
- 1 teaspoon vanilla extract
- $^1/_4$ cup oats
- 6-8 ice cubes

INSTRUCTIONS

1. Add everything into a high-speed blender and blend for 1 minute.

2. Serve over ice or as is.

Jazz's Tricks!

Add a handful of frozen cauliflower florets for added fiber and creamy consistency.

Add 1 scoop of vanilla protein powder for additional protein.

Substitute the flax seeds for chia seeds or hemp seeds.

PEANUT BUTTER BANANA SMOOTHIE

Yield: 1 Serving | Total time: 5 Min

INGREDIENTS

- 1 banana, frozen
- 1/2 cup frozen cauliflower florets
- 1 cup plant-based milk (almond, oat, or coconut milk)
- 2 tablespoons peanut butter
- 1 serving chocolate protein powder
- 1 tablespoon flax seeds
- $^1/_2$ teaspoon ground cinnamon
- 4-6 ice cubes
- 1 tablespoon honey or maple syrup (optional for added sweetness)
- 1/2 teaspoon vanilla extract

INSTRUCTIONS

1. Add everything into a high-speed blender and blend for 1 minute.
2. Serve over ice or as is.

Jazz's Tricks!

The more brown the banana, the sweeter it is!

To freeze your bananas, remove the skin then store in a bag or airtight container in the freezer. They make the best smoothie addition for creaminess and sweetness.

Use any nut or seed butter on hand. Try swapping the almond butter for peanut butter! Swap the flax seeds for chia seeds or hemp seeds!

Add a handful of fresh spinach for extra greens (you won't taste a thing)!

Appetizers & Sides

A quick and easy way to impress!

When it comes to hosting, I like to keep things simple without sacrificing flavor. That's why I've taken inspiration from some of my favorite restaurant appetizers and turned them into quick, easy, and beginner-friendly recipes. Whether you're serving up classic crowd-pleasers like Air Fryer Chicken Wings or something a little different like Tortellini Antipasto Sticks, these appetizers will have your guests thinking you spent hours in the kitchen—when in reality, they come together in no time. Hosting just got a whole lot easier!

CREAMY WHIPPED COTTAGE CHEESE

Yield: 6-8 | Total Time: 5 Min

This is inspired by my favorite Middle Eastern restaurant in my hometown of Santa Barbara, California. It was served as an appetizer with some fresh bread for dipping. Great for easy entertaining!

INGREDIENTS

- 2 cups cottage cheese
- 1 teaspoon garlic powder
- 1 tablespoon olive oil
- 1/4 cup pomegranate seeds
- 1/4 cup chopped pistachios
- Pinch of flaky salt
- Crackers (for serving)

INSTRUCTIONS

1. Whip the cottage cheese and garlic powder in a food processor for 2 minutes until smooth and creamy, scraping down the sides if necessary. Taste & make any adjustments with seasonings!
2. Pour into bowl and drizzle with olive oil, pomegranate seeds, chopped pistachios and flakey salt.
3. Serve with crackers for dipping!

TGI FRIDAYS LOADED POTATO SKINS

Yield: 8 Potato Skins | Total Time: 30 Min

I make these when we are watching football rooting for the Tampa Bay Buccaneers on Sundays! My husband is always so excited when he sees these in the air fryer!

INGREDIENTS

- 4 small russet potatoes
- 1 tablespoon olive oil
- 1/4 teaspoon salt
- 1/4 teaspoon pepper
- 1/4 teaspoon paprika

Toppings

- 1/2 cup grated cheddar cheese
- 2 tablespoons bacon bits
- 1 green onion, sliced on a bias
- 1/4 cup sour cream
- 1 tablespoon cilantro, chopped

INSTRUCTIONS

1. Wash your potatoes and dry them off. Prick the skins 5 times all over with a fork.

2. Place the potatoes on a microwave-safe plate. Microwave for 8 minutes, turning the potatoes over halfway. Once the potatoes are squishy on the outside, they are cooked! Remove them carefully from the microwave and set them in the fridge to cool completely. Note: 8 minutes works for 4 inch potatoes. If you have larger potatoes, you may need to cook for longer.

3. Once they are cooled completely, cut each potato lengthwise and use a small spoon to scoop out the flesh.

4. To the potato skins, add a drizzle of olive oil, then a sprinkle of salt, pepper, and paprika to the inside. Rub it in with your hands.

5. Place the potatoes hollow side up in the air fryer.

6. Air fry at 360F for 7 minutes.

7. Open the air fryer basket and top the potato skins with cheese, bacon bites and green onions.

8. Air fry at 360F for another 3 minutes or until cheese is melted.

9. Drizzle with sour cream and sprinkle with cilantro, then serve!

COPYCAT CHEESECAKE FACTORY SPINACH ARTICHOKE DIP

Prep Time: 5 Min | Total Time: 20 Min

We used to go to The Cheesecake Factory for my husband's birthday every single year and we would always get this appetizer. I created this version because it swaps out heavy ingredients like mayonnaise and heavy cream for a blend of Greek yogurt, cream cheese, and sour cream, and no one has noticed a difference!

INGREDIENTS

- 4 oz cream cheese, at room temperature
- 1/2 cup Greek yogurt
- 1/3 cup sour cream
- 1/2 cup mozzarella cheese, shredded (divided into 1/4 cup portions)
- 1/4 cup parmesan cheese, shredded
- 3/4 cup frozen spinach, thawed and squeezed to remove excess liquid
- 1 14 oz can artichoke hearts, drained
- 5 cloves garlic, minced
- 3/4 teaspoon salt
- 3/4 teaspoon black pepper
- Crackers or bread (for dipping)

INSTRUCTIONS

1. Roughly chop the drained artichoke hearts. The pieces don't need to be uniform —rather just small enough so that no one ends up with a large chunk of artichoke in their bite.

2. Add the cream cheese, greek yogurt, sour cream, 1/4 cup mozzarella cheese and parmesan cheese to a large bowl and stir well to combine.

3. Transfer to an air fryer-safe ramekin and sprinkle with the remaining 1/4 cup of mozzarella cheese.

4. Air fry at 350F for 15 mins, until the cheese melts on top.

5. Remove from the air fryer carefully and let it cool for about 10 minutes before serving.

6. Use your favorite crackers or bread for dipping!

JALAPEÑO POPPERS IN THE AIR FRYER

Yield: 16 | Total Time: 20 Min

Every single year, my mom makes the absolute best jalapeño poppers for Christmas Eve. This is her recipe, with a little twist to make them lighter but just as creamy.

INGREDIENTS

- 8 large jalapeños, cut in half, seeds removed
- 3/4 cup Greek yogurt
- 1/4 cup extra-sharp cheddar cheese, finely grated
- ¼ cup chopped fresh cilantro, plus 1 tablespoon for garnish
- ¼ cup chopped green onion, plus 1 tablespoon for garnish
- ½ teaspoon salt
- ¼ teaspoon black pepper
- ½ teaspoon onion powder
- 1/2 teaspoon garlic powder
- 1/8 teaspoon paprika
- 1 tablespoon olive oil
- 2 tablespoons cooked crumbled bacon

INSTRUCTIONS

1. To prepare the jalapeños, wash them thoroughly and cut them in half lengthwise. Remove the seeds—wearing food-grade gloves is recommended to avoid irritation, as jalapeño seeds are very spicy. Dispose of the gloves after use. It's also important to wash your hands, knife, cutting board, and any surfaces touched by the jalapeños. Even after washing, residual oils can cause irritation.

2. In a large bowl, combine the Greek yogurt, finely grated cheddar cheese, fresh chopped cilantro, sliced green onion, salt, pepper, onion powder, garlic powder and paprika. Mix well to combine.

3. Stuff each jalapeño half with a scoop of filling.

4. Preheat the air fryer to 380F.

5. Place the jalapeños, filling side up in the air fryer. Drizzle with olive oil.

6. Air fry at 380 F for 10 minutes, until the filling is golden brown.

7. Sprinkle with crumbled bacon, extra cilantro, and green onion. Serve as a snack!

QUICK AND EASY MANGO SALSA

Yield: 3 cups | Total Time: 15 Min

I can never make enough of this salsa. By the time it's chopped and served, its already gone.

INGREDIENTS

- 1 ripe mango, diced
- 1 red bell pepper, diced
- 1/2 red onion, diced
- 1 jalapeño, seeds removed and diced
- Juice of 1 lime
- 1/4 cup chopped cilantro
- 1/2 teaspoon salt
- 1/4 teaspoon black pepper
- 2 tablespoons olive oil

INSTRUCTIONS

1. To prepare the jalapeños, wash them thoroughly and cut them in half lengthwise. Remove the seeds—wearing food-grade gloves is recommended to avoid irritation, as jalapeño seeds are very spicy. Dispose of the gloves after use. It's also important to wash your hands, knife, cutting board, and any surfaces touched by the jalapeños. Even after washing, residual oils can cause irritation. In a medium bowl, combine the diced mango, red bell pepper, red onion, and jalapeño.
2. Add the lime juice, chopped cilantro, salt, and pepper.
3. Drizzle the olive oil over the salsa and mix until well combined.

CRISPY AIR FRYER SALT & PEPPER CHICKEN WINGS

Yield: 8-10 pieces | Total Time: 35 Min

My husband doesn't know the difference between his wings deep fried or air fried. So air fry them using this recipe and save on the oil!

INGREDIENTS

- 1 lb chicken wings, party style
- 2 teaspoons cornstarch
- 1 teaspoon salt
- 1 teaspoon black pepper
- 2 tablespoons fresh parsley, for garnish
- Avocado oil spray

INSTRUCTIONS

1. Preheat the air fryer to 375F degrees.
2. Pat the chicken dry really well.
3. Sprinkle with cornstarch, salt and pepper. Toss with your hands to coat each wing.
4. Spray wings with avocado oil spray.
5. Place the chicken wings in the air fryer basket and air fry at 375F for 15 minutes.
6. Flip wings, increase temperature to 400F and cook for an additional 15 minutes until the wings are crisp and cooked through. The internal temperature should be 165F.

CRISPY AIR FRYER ZUCCHINI FRIES

Serves: 4 People | Total Time: 25 Min

INGREDIENTS

- 2 medium zucchini
- Avocado oil spray

Wet Ingredients

- 2 large eggs

Dry Ingredients

- 1 cup breadcrumbs
- 1/2 cup grated parmesan cheese
- 3/4 teaspoon paprika
- 3/4 teaspoon garlic powder
- 1/2 teaspoon salt
- 1/4 teaspoon pepper

My mom and I were obsessed with the Carls Jr. zucchini fries so I decided to make a version of their fries, just lighter and not deep fried. This tastes just like the fast food restaurant but crispier!

INSTRUCTIONS

1. Preheat your air fryer to 400F.
2. Cut the zucchini into long, thin strips (resembling fries).
3. In one shallow bowl, whisk the eggs.
4. In another shallow bowl, combine the breadcrumbs, parmesan cheese, paprika, garlic powder, salt and pepper. Mix well.
5. Spray your air fryer with avocado oil spray.
6. Dip the zucchini fries into the egg mixture, then the breadcrumb mixture. Shake off any excess breading. Place them in the air fryer in a single layer, careful not to overcrowd.
7. Air fry at 400F for 18 minutes, flipping them halfway through.
8. Serve the fries immediately with your favorite dipping sauce or marinara!

AIR FRYER CARROT FRIES

Serves: 4 People | Total Time: 30 Min

INGREDIENTS

- 1 lb large carrots, washed and peeled
- 1 tablespoon avocado oil
- 1 tablespoon cornstarch
- 1 teaspoon garlic powder
- 1/2 cup grated parmesan cheese (divided into 1/4 cups)
- 1/2 teaspoon salt
- 1/2 teaspoon black pepper
- 1/4 teaspoon crushed red pepper

The first time I made these everyone was hesitant, but as soon as they dug in, no one could stop! It's a greet way to use up a huge bag of carrots you have!

INSTRUCTIONS

1. Remove the tops from one large carrot. Cut the carrot in half crosswise, then slice each half lengthwise. Next, slice each piece lengthwise again, so you have quarters. From the thicker end, cut 3 strips, and from the thinner end, cut 2 strips. Try to keep all the strips similar in size to ensure even cooking.

2. In a bowl, mix together the cornstarch, 1/4 cup of parmesan cheese, garlic powder, salt, black pepper and crushed red pepper flakes.

3. Drizzle the carrots with avocado oil and toss to coat. Add the seasoning mixture and toss to coat again.

4. Add the carrot fries to an air fryer basket in an even layer, careful not to overlap. Sprinkle the remainder of 1/4 cup parmesan cheese to the top of the carrots.

   Note: It's important to make sure they are in a single layer.

5. Air fry at 350F for 20-22 minutes. Finish with chopped parsley and add your favorite dip on the side!

EASY HOMEMADE PEPPERONI PIZZA ROLLS

Yield: 4 Pizza Rolls | Total Time: 15 Min

When I was in high school, pizza rolls were my favorite snack. Every time my friends came over, we popped them in the microwave. This is a much better version, the air fryer melts the cheese to make it gooey and the outside stays crispy! I love dipping in marinara!

INGREDIENTS

- 4 tortillas (about 6″-8″ size)
- 1/2 cup pizza sauce
- 1/2 cup mozzarella cheese, shredded
- 20 pieces of pepperoni
- 4 string cheese
- Avocado oil spray
- 1/4 teaspoon dried garlic powder
- 1/4 teaspoon dried oregano

INSTRUCTIONS

1. Lay all of your tortillas flat on a cutting board.
2. Spread about 1-2 tablespoons of pizza sauce on each tortilla, making sure to spread evenly.
3. Sprinkle evenly with about 1 tablespoon of shredded mozzarella cheese.
4. Line 5 slices of pepperoni down the middle.
5. Place the string cheese in the center on top of the pepperoni.

6. Roll the tortilla as tight as you can and place it seam side down in your sprayed air fryer basket.
7. Repeat with all of the tortillas.
8. Place in the air fryer at 350F for 10 minutes, flipping halfway.
9. Let them cool for a few minutes before diving in.
10. Serve with your favorite pizza sauce for dipping.

BUFFALO CAULIFLOWER RECIPE WITH RANCH DIP

Yield: 2-4 Servings | Total Time: 45 Min

I would make this for my non-meat eating friends when they came over. Everyone always loved the flavor and thought it was the perfect alternative to buffalo chicken wings!

INGREDIENTS

- 1 12 oz bag cauliflower florets
- 1 egg
- 1 1/2 cup almond flour
- 1 teaspoon garlic powder
- 1/2 teaspoon salt
- 1/2 teaspoon paprika
- 1 cup buffalo sauce
- healthy homemade ranch (see page 180)

INSTRUCTIONS

1. Preheat your air fryer at 400F for 4 minutes.

2. In a large bowl, whisk 1 egg. Add the cauliflower florets and mix well for a minute until the cauliflower is evenly coated in the egg.

3. In a small bowl, combine the almond flour, garlic powder, salt and paprika. Add the mixture into the bowl with the egg and cauliflower and mix to coat well.

4. Spray your air fryer with avocado oil spray. Place the cauliflower in the preheated air fryer in a single layer. Air fry at 400F for 12 minutes, shaking half way.

5. Remove the air fried cauliflower from the air fryer, add it into a big bowl along with the buffalo sauce. Toss to coat then transfer back into the air fryer for an additional 6 minutes.

AIR FRYER SHISHITO PEPPERS

Serves: 2-3 People | Total Time: 10 Min

INGREDIENTS

- 8 ounces shishito peppers, washed and dried
- 2 teaspoons avocado oil
- 1/2 teaspoon salt

Sauce

- 1/3 cup mayonnaise
- 2 tablespoons lemon juice
- 1/2 teaspoon paprika
- 1/2 teaspoon garlic powder
- 1/4 teaspoon salt

Every time I go out to eat with my mom, she orders the shishito peppers as an appetizer, so I created this for her. Now I make it for her every time she comes over.

INSTRUCTIONS

1. Preheat your air fryer to 400F.
2. Toss the peppers with avocado oil and salt until evenly coated.
3. Place into your air fryer layer basket in an even layer. Cook for 9 minutes, shaking half way through.
4. While the peppers are roasting, make the dipping sauce by combining mayonnaise, lemon juice, paprika and garlic powder. Stir until smooth.
5. Transfer the peppers on a plate with the dipping sauce. Serve immediately.

TORTELLINI ANTIPASTO STICKS

Yield: 4 Servings | Total time: 20 Min

INGREDIENTS

- 1 package (9 ounces) of tortellini pasta, any kind
- 4 ounces of thinly sliced salami
- 8 small mozzarella balls
- 6 slices of provolone cheese, cut into quarters
- 1 cup of roasted marinated bell peppers, sliced into 1 inch bite-sized pieces
- 1 cup of jarred artichoke hearts, drained and halved
- 1 cup of cherry tomatoes, halved
- 2 tablespoons of olive oil
- 1 tablespoon of fresh lemon juice
- 2 tablespoons of fresh parsley, chopped
- ¼ teaspoon salt
- ¼ teaspoon pepper

INSTRUCTIONS

1. Cook the tortellini pasta according to the package instructions until al dente. My tip is to cook them about 2 minutes shy of al dente as you don't want them mushy on the skewer. Drain and set aside to cool.

2. Assemble your skewers: Thread one piece of tortellini pasta onto the skewer, followed by a folded slice of salami, a mozzarella ball, a quarter slice of provolone, a piece of roasted bell pepper, half of an artichoke heart, and a cherry tomato half. Repeat until the skewer is full, leaving a little space at the top for easy handling. You can do it in any order you prefer! Have fun with it.

3. Repeat the process until you have assembled all your skewers.

4. Arrange the skewers on a serving platter.

5. In a small bowl, whisk together some olive oil, fresh lemon juice, salt and pepper to make a simple dressing.

6. Drizzle the olive oil and lemon juice dressing over the skewers.

7. Sprinkle the chopped fresh parsley as a garnish.

Jazz's Tricks!

You can prep these up to 24 hours in advance and keep them chilled in the refrigerator. Hold off on the dressing and fresh parsley until you are ready to serve.

Salads

Simple, satisfying and never boring

In my kitchen, salads are never an afterthought. These are my tried-and-true recipes, bursting with nutrients to stand alone as a meal or complement your favorite protein. Whether it's a quick lunch or a fresh addition to dinner, these salads always deliver. From crisp and refreshing to hearty and satisfying, they'll keep your table exciting and anything but boring!

TIKTOK GREEN GODDESS SALAD

Serves: 6 People | Total Time: 30 Min

This salad was trending on TikTok and I saw people use it as a dip for chips. I thought that was genius! We love making this as a quick lunch in our house.

INGREDIENTS

- 1 head of cabbage, preferably organic
- 6 Persian cucumbers
- 1/2 bunch green onions, about 3/4 cup chopped
- 1 pomegranate
- 1 lemon
- 1/4 cup chives, chopped
- 1/4 teaspoon salt
- 1/4 teaspoon pepper

Dressing Ingredients

- see page 182

INSTRUCTIONS

1. Add all of the ingredients for the green goddess salad dressing into a high-powered blender. Start with 1/2 cup water and add more if needed to thin out. Blend for 30 seconds until creamy and smooth. Pour into a mason jar & set aside.

2. Cut the cabbage in 4 parts. If using a food processor, add the cabbage in the food processor and pulse about 3-4 times until cabbage is chopped. Transfer into a big bowl & continue to pulse the cabbage until all of it is used.

3. Dice the Persian cucumbers, slice the green onion, and chives. Add it into the salad. Add the salt & pepper, and mix to combine.

4. Add the pomegranate seeds to the salad. See instructions below.

5. Store the dressing & the salad separately and toss the dressing into the salad when you're ready to eat!

STEP FOR THE POMEGRANATE

1. Begin by carefully slicing off the crown (the flower end) of the pomegranate to reveal the inner sections and white membranes that separate the seeds. You'll notice several white lines running from the top to the bottom of the fruit; these indicate the natural divisions.

2. Using a sharp knife, make shallow cuts along each of these white lines from the top to the base, being cautious not to cut too deep into the seeds.

3. Once all the lines are scored, gently pry the pomegranate apart with your hands into separate segments. This will expose the seeds, which can easily be loosened and removed by gently rubbing or tapping the back of each segment over a bowl. This method helps keep the seeds intact and reduces the amount of juice splatter, making for a cleaner and more efficient deseeding process.

COPYCAT CHICK-FIL-A COBB SALAD

Yield: 4 servings | Total Time: 40 Min

INGREDIENTS

For the Salad:

- 6 cups lettuce of choice, chopped
- 1 cup tomatoes, diced
- 1 cup charred corn (about 1 ear of corn)
- 1/2 cup turkey bacon or bacon of choice, cooked and chopped
- 2 hard-boiled eggs, peeled and chopped
- 1/2 cup Monterey Jack cheese, shredded
- 1/2 cup sharp cheddar cheese, shredded
- 1 1/2 cups copycat Chick-fil-A air-fried nuggets (recipe below)
- Avocado ranch (see page 190)

Every time we go travel through airports, this is our go-to salad from Chik-fil-A! I love making a big batch for meal prep for the week.

For the Copycat Chick-fil-A Nuggets:

- 1 lb chicken breast, cut into 1-inch cubes
- 1 cup dill pickle juice
- 1 egg, whisked
- 1/2 cup milk of choice
- 1 cup flour of choice
- 2 teaspoons salt
- 1 teaspoon pepper
- 1 teaspoon paprika

INSTRUCTIONS

Prepare the Chicken Nuggets:

1. Marinate the Chicken: Place the chicken breast cubes in a bowl and pour the dill pickle juice over them. Cover and refrigerate for at least 30 minutes, up to 24 hours.

2. Prepare the Coating: After marinating, add the whisked egg and milk to the same bowl with the chicken. Mix well.

3. Coat the Chicken: In another bowl, combine the flour, salt, pepper, and paprika. Remove the chicken cubes from the wet mixture and coat them in the dry flour mixture. Shake off any excess coating.

4. Air Fry: Spray the air fryer basket with avocado oil or olive oil spray. Place the chicken nuggets in a single layer, working in batches if necessary. Spray the tops of the chicken nuggets with oil spray. Air fry at 380°F for about 15 minutes, flipping the nuggets halfway through.

Prep the Salad Ingredients:

5. Wash and dry your lettuce, then chop it into bite-sized pieces.

6. Dice the tomatoes, char your corn on a stovetop or grill, and cook the turkey bacon in a skillet or air fryer until crispy. Chop the bacon into small pieces.

7. Prepare your hard-boiled eggs by boiling them, cooling them under cold water, peeling, and chopping them.

Assemble the Salad:

8. In a large bowl, layer the chopped lettuce, tomatoes, charred corn, chopped turkey bacon, hard-boiled eggs, shredded Monterey Jack, and sharp cheddar cheese.

9. Top the salad with your homemade Chick-fil-A air-fried nuggets.

SERVE:

Drizzle the avocado ranch dressing over the salad, toss gently, and enjoy your homemade Chick-fil-A Cobb Salad!

ROASTED SWEET POTATO AND KALE FALL SALAD WITH MAPLE VINAIGRETTE

Yield: 4 Servings | Total Time: 30 Min

If I had to choose one thing to eat for the rest of my life, believe it or not, this would be it. The combination is incredible. In the fall, I have this salad non-stop. The leftovers are even better!

INGREDIENTS

For the Salad:

- 2 medium-sized sweet potatoes, peeled and diced into 1/2-inch cubes
- 1 bunch of kale, stems removed and leaves torn into bite-sized pieces
- 2 apples, thinly sliced (use your favorite variety)
- 1/2 cup crumbled goat cheese
- 1/2 cup pecan halves, toasted
- 1/2 cup dried cranberries

For the Maple Vinaigrette:

- 1/4 cup extra-virgin olive oil
- 2 tablespoons apple cider vinegar
- 1 tablespoon pure maple syrup
- 1 teaspoon Dijon mustard
- Salt and black pepper to taste

INSTRUCTIONS

Prepare the Sweet Potatoes in the Air Fryer

1. In a bowl, toss the diced sweet potatoes with a drizzle of olive oil, salt, and pepper to coat them evenly.

2. Place the sweet potatoes in the air fryer basket in a single layer. You may need to cook them in batches depending on the size of your air fryer.

3. Air fry at 400°F for about 15-20 minutes, shaking the basket halfway through, or until the sweet potatoes are tender and slightly crispy. Adjust the time as needed based on your air fryer's performance.

4. Prepare the Maple Vinaigrette:

5. In a mason jar with a lid or a small bowl, add the olive oil, apple cider vinegar, maple syrup, Dijon mustard, salt, and pepper. Shake until combined.

6. Massage the Kale:

7. Place the torn kale leaves in a large bowl. Drizzle a little bit of the maple vinaigrette over the kale. Use your hands to gently massage the vinaigrette into the kale leaves for about 2-3 minutes. This helps to soften the kale and make it more tender.

8. Assemble the Salad:

9. Add the air-fried sweet potatoes to the massaged kale.

10. Scatter the sliced apples, crumbled goat cheese, toasted pecans, and dried cranberries over the top.

11. Drizzle the remaining maple vinaigrette over the salad.

12. Gently toss all the ingredients together until they are well coated with the dressing.

13. Serve immediately as a side dish or add grilled chicken or another protein of your choice for a complete meal.

COPYCAT CHICK-FIL-A MARKET SALAD

Yield: 2 Servings | Total Time: 10 Min

This is my favorite salad from Chick-fil-A—I love fruit on my salad! Whenever I am low on time, I make this salad for my husband and me. We both love how fresh it tastes, with the slight creaminess from the blue cheese.

INGREDIENTS

- 4-6 cups spring mix
- ⅓ cup strawberries, sliced
- ¼ cup Granny Smith apples, diced
- ¼ cup blueberries
- ¼ cup walnuts, chopped
- 2 chicken breasts, air fried (see page 155)
- ¼ cup blue cheese
- ¼ cup granola

Apple Cider Vinaigrette

- 1/2 cup olive oil
- 1/4 cup apple cider vinaigrette
- 1 lime, juiced
- 2 tablespoon honey
- 1/4 teaspoon salt
- 1/4 teaspoon black pepper
- ¼ teaspoon garlic powder

INSTRUCTIONS

1. Begin by making the chicken! You can use my air-fried chicken cutlet recipe (see page 155).
2. Grab a big bowl, and add the spring mix to the bottom.
3. Add the strawberries, apples, blueberries, walnuts, blue cheese and granola on top.
4. Into a jar with a lid, add the ingredients for the apple cider vinaigrette. Shake it well to combine. Taste and make any adjustments if needed.
5. Finish the salad with sliced chicken and a drizzle of apple cider vinaigrette.
6. Toss to combine & enjoy right away.

TRADER JOE'S YEAR-ROUND SALAD

Yield: 6 Servings | Total Time: 15 Min

If I am ever invited to a gathering, I offer to bring a salad. This is the salad I bring every single time. It's easy to make, the crunch always adds an extra element and everyone loves it!

INGREDIENTS

- 6 cups spring mix
- 4 cups arugula
- 1 cup red grapes, chopped
- 1 cup apple, chopped
- 3/4 cup feta cheese
- 1/3 cup pumpkin seeds, toasted
- 1/3 cup walnuts, toasted & chopped
- 1/4 cup unsweetened dried cherries

Balsamic Dressing

- 1/4 cup balsamic vinegar
- 1/4 cup olive oil
- 1/4 cup spicy Dijon mustard
- 1/2 teaspoon salt
- 1/2 teaspoon pepper
- 1/2 teaspoon garlic powder

INSTRUCTIONS

1. Combine all of the ingredients in a large bowl.

2. Add all of the ingredients of the dressing into a mason jar, small blender, or bowl. Shake, blend or whisk well until it's all blended. Toss the salad with the homemade balsamic Dijon vinaigrette. Serve immediately.

Jazz's Tips

1. To toast the nuts and seeds, just place them on a non-stick pan for about 5 minutes on medium heat to warm. Stir a few times to keep them from burning.

Substitutions

1. Use any greens for the spring mix and arugula. This is also really good with romaine or butter lettuce.

2. Try green grapes instead of red.

3. Try gorgonzola cheese or blue cheese instead of feta.

4. Any nuts and seeds would work in place of the pumpkin and walnuts. I love sliced almonds, pecans, and sunflower seeds as well.

5. Try dried cranberries instead of dried cherries.

WATERMELON CUCUMBER SALAD WITH FETA RECIPE

Yield: 4-6 Servings | Total Time: 15 Min

This Persian Watermelon Feta Salad is often what we eat for breakfast. It is often served with some fresh toasted lavash bread, especially on a hot summer day.

INGREDIENTS

- 1 mini watermelon, cubed
- 6 Persian cucumbers, chopped
- 8 oz feta cheese, cubed or crumbled
- ¼ cup pistachios, chopped
- ¼ cup mint, sliced into ribbons
- 1 large lime, zested and juiced
- 1 teaspoon flaky sea salt

INSTRUCTIONS

1. Place the watermelon, cucumber, and feta cheese in a large mixing bowl.
2. Add the chopped pistachios and mint to the bowl with the salad.
3. Add the lime zest and juice to the bowl.
4. Sprinkle the salad with flaky salt and mix well to combine the ingredients. Taste and make any needed adjustments.
5. This gets better over time, so feel free to leave it in the fridge to chill for 30-60 minutes before serving.

WARM GOAT CHEESE KALE SALAD

Yield: 2 Servings | Total Time: 35 minutes

INGREDIENTS

Base

- 6 cups chopped kale
- 8 carrots, washed and peeled
- 4 pre-cooked beets, chopped
- 4 figs, sliced
- 3 oz of goat cheese, in a log
- 1 pomegranate, seeded
- 1/4 cup walnuts, toasted
- 2 teaspoons avocado oil (divided)
- 1/8 teaspoon salt
- 1/8 teaspoon pepper

Dressing

- 1/4 cup extra virgin olive oil
- 1/4 cup red wine vinegar
- 1 lemon, juiced
- 1 teaspoon honey
- 1/4 teaspoon salt
- 1/4 teaspoon black pepper

I recreated the best salad I ever ate, and it was from Monaco! Here's my version of the salad we ordered in Europe, the creamy cheese and light dressing are the perfect combination!

INSTRUCTIONS

1. Preheat the oven to 425 degrees Fahrenheit.

2. Place the carrots on a parchment paper lined sheet pan, toss with 1 teaspoon of avocado oil, salt, and pepper—roast for about 30 minutes.

3. Chop the kale into small pieces. Set aside in a bowl while you prepare the dressing.

4. Slice the goat cheese into 1 tablespoon-size rounds and place them flat on a plate with plastic wrap. Place them in the fridge to firm for about 20 minutes.

5. Add all of the dressing ingredients into a mason jar with a lid and shake well until combined. Pour about 1/2 of the dressing onto the kale and thoroughly massage with your fingers to get into all of the leaves. This should take about 60 seconds. Set your massaged kale aside to marinate while the rest of the ingredients come together.

6. When you are ready to grill the cheese, add 1 teaspoon of avocado oil into a non-stick pan on high heat. Once the pan is hot, add in your goat cheese rounds and cook for about 60 seconds to 90 seconds on each side until a slight caramelization occurs. You can keep these in the pan until you are ready to plate.

7. Serve the massaged kale with roasted carrots, roasted sliced beets, warmed goat cheese, pomegranate, walnuts, and dressing on top.

PERSIAN SHIRAZI SALAD

Yield: 4 servings | Total Time: 20 Min

INGREDIENTS

- 2 large tomatoes, diced
- 2 Persian cucumbers, diced
- 1/2 red onion, finely chopped
- 1/4 cup fresh parsley, chopped
- 1/4 cup fresh mint, chopped
- Juice of 2 lemons, about ¼ cup lemon juice
- 2 tablespoons olive oil
- 1 teaspoon salt
- 1 teaspoon pepper
- 1/2 teaspoon garlic powder

INSTRUCTIONS

1. In a large salad bowl, combine the diced tomatoes, diced Persian cucumbers, chopped red onion, chopped parsley, and chopped mint.

2. Add the lemon juice, olive oil, salt, pepper, and garlic powder to the fresh salad.

3. Gently toss to coat the vegetables evenly.

4. Optional to chill the salad for 10 minutes to marinate. Note: this salad gets better over time.

Jazz's Tricks!

- Store the salad in the fridge for up to 3 days. Enjoy chilled.
- The salad gets better as it marinates in the fridge. If time allows, let it sit for 30 minutes before serving.
- If fresh herbs (mint and parsley) are not available, use dried!

QUICK AND EASY CHICKPEA TUNA SALAD RECIPE

Yield: 4-6 Serving | Total Time: 15 Min

My husband's favorite food is tuna. So whenever he is craving it, I make a big batch of this tuna salad for us to eat on salads, sandwiches, in wraps or with crackers.

INGREDIENTS

- 2 cans (5 oz each) of chunk tuna in water, drained
- 1 can of chickpeas, drained and rinsed
- 1/4 red onion, about 1/4 cup diced
- 1/4 cup celery, diced
- 2 tablespoons capers, drained and chopped
- 2 tablespoons granulated onion
- 2 tablespoons mayo or Greek yogurt
- 1 tablespoon Dijon mustard or spicy mustard
- 2 lemons, juiced
- 1 tablespoon granulated garlic
- salt and pepper to taste

INSTRUCTIONS

1. Add all of the ingredients into a bowl. Mix well to combine!
2. Taste to make any adjustments.
3. Serve on a piece of toasted bread, with crackers or on a salad.

JAZZ'S HOUSE SALAD WITH BALSAMIC DIJON DRESSING

Yield: 2 Servings | Total time: 10 Min

SALAD INGREDIENTS:

- 5 cups spring mix salad greens
- 1 cup cherry tomatoes, halved
- 2 Persian cucumbers, thinly sliced
- salt and pepper, to taste

Balsamic Dijon Dressing Ingredients:

- 2 tablespoons Dijon mustard
- 1/2 cup olive oil
- 1/4 cup balsamic vinegar
- Juice of 1/2 lemon
- 1 tablespoon honey or maple syrup
- 1/4 teaspoon salt
- 1/4 teaspoon black pepper
- 1/4 teaspoon garlic powder

INSTRUCTIONS

1. In a mason jar with a lid, combine Dijon mustard, olive oil, balsamic vinegar, lemon juice, honey or maple syrup, salt, pepper, and garlic powder. Put the lid on and shake until mixed well. Alternatively, you can whisk in a small bowl.

2. In a large salad bowl, combine spring mix salad greens, cherry tomatoes, and Persian cucumbers. Season the salad with salt and pepper to taste. Toss gently to distribute the seasoning evenly. This is the most important step!

3. Drizzle the prepared Balsamic Dijon Dressing over the salad, starting with a few tablespoons and adding more as desired. Toss the salad gently to coat all ingredients with the dressing. Serve the salad immediately!

VIBRANT SUMAC SUPER SALAD

Yield: 2-4 Servings | Total Time: 20 Min

INGREDIENTS

- 6 cups mixed greens
- 3 large carrots, shredded
- 1 avocado, sliced
- 2 tomatoes, chopped
- 1 apple, chopped
- 1 can (15 oz) chickpeas, drained and rinsed
- 2 tablespoons dried cranberries
- 1/2 large cucumber, sliced
- 1/4 cup raw nuts or seeds
- Fresh herbs (mint, parsley, dill, or cilantro)
- 1/2 teaspoon sumac
- 1/2 cup cooked quinoa
- Balsamic vinaigrette dressing (see dressings page 178)

INSTRUCTIONS

1. In a large bowl, add the mixed greens and a pinch of salt. Toss.

2. Add the carrots, avocado, tomato, apple, chickpeas, dried cranberries, cucumber, nuts, herbs, quinoa, and sumac.

3. Drizzle with the balsamic vinaigrette dressing. Toss everything together until well combined.

Jazz's Tricks!

Sumac is a tangy, lemony spice made from dried and ground berries, commonly used in Middle Eastern and Mediterranean cuisine. It adds a bright, citrusy flavor to dishes and is often sprinkled on salads, meats, and dips for an extra zing. You can source sumac from Middle Eastern markets or online!

PEACH AND BASIL SALAD

Yield: 2 Servings | Total Time: 15 Min

INGREDIENTS

- 2 ripe peaches, halved and pitted
- 4 cups salad greens
- 1/2 cup crumbled goat cheese
- 1/4 cup basil, finely sliced
- 1/4 cup sliced almonds
- 3 tablespoons balsamic vinegar
- 2 tablespoons olive oil
- 1 teaspoon honey
- ⅛ teaspoon salt (more to taste)
- ⅛ teaspoon pepper (more to taste)

INSTRUCTIONS

1. Into a large bowl, add your spring mix, chopped peaches, basil, nuts and goat cheese.
2. Drizzle with balsamic vinegar, olive oil, honey, salt and pepper to taste.
3. Give it a quick toss & serve as a side to your favorite protein!

WARM KALE & BRUSSELS CRUNCH SALAD

Yield: 4 Servings | Total Time: 15 Min

INGREDIENTS

- 16 oz sliced and pre-washed Brussels sprouts
- 2 tablespoons olive oil (divided)
- 1 (12 oz) bag pre-washed, pre-chopped kale
- 12 oz cherry tomatoes, halved
- 6 Persian cucumbers, chopped
- 1/2 teaspoon salt
- 1/2 teaspoon pepper
- 5 scallions, thinly sliced on a bias
- 1/2 bunch cilantro, chopped
- 1 (15 oz) can cannellini beans
- Caramelized Shallot Magic Sauce (see page 184)

INSTRUCTIONS

1. Heat a medium non-stick skillet over medium-high heat.
2. Add 1 tablespoon of olive oil. Once the oil is hot, add the sliced Brussels sprouts.
3. Stir for about 5 minutes until the Brussels sprouts are slightly charred. Remove from heat and transfer to a bowl.
4. In a large bowl, add the pre-washed kale with 1 tablespoon of olive oil. Massage the olive oil into the kale to break it down. Spend about 90 seconds massaging the kale.
5. Once the kale is massaged in oil, add the charred Brussels sprouts, cherry tomatoes, and chopped cucumber. Season with 1/2 teaspoon salt and 1/2 teaspoon pepper. Toss gently to mix.
6. Drizzle the Caramelized Shallot Magic Sauce over the salad. Start with half of the dressing and toss to combine. Add more dressing if desired.
7. To serve, add scallions and cilantro.

Jazz's Tricks!

Swap the beans for any beans on hand like chickpeas or kidney beans.

For some added flavor, add crumbled bacon, turkey bacon or any sort of toasted nut or seed to this salad for an additional crunch.

Store leftover salad in an airtight container in the refrigerator for up to 3 days. The dressing can be stored separately for up to 1 week.

Pasta & Pizza

My all-time favorite comfort foods

Pizza and pasta are my ultimate comfort foods—I could eat them every single day and never get bored! This collection is all about taking the rich, satisfying flavors I adore and making them approachable for anyone. I've simplified the process without sacrificing taste, so you can whip up comforting, cozy meals with ease. Dive in and discover why these recipes are my go-to for effortless, delicious dishes that always hit the spot.

COOKBOOK / COOKBOOK / COOKBOOK / COOKBOOK /

AIR FRYER ARGENTINIAN SHRIMP WITH GREEN GODDESS PASTA

Yield: 4 servings | Total Time: 19 Min

Postpartum, I lived for creamy pastas that were easy to make. I made my husband make this recipe for me at least once a week. It was easy enough for him to make without feeling overwhelmed!

INGREDIENTS

Shrimp Ingredients

- 1 lb Argentinian red shrimp, peeled and deveined
- 2 tablespoons extra virgin olive oil
- 1 teaspoon garlic powder
- 1 teaspoon paprika
- 1 teaspoon salt
- 1/2 teaspoon black pepper
- 1/2 teaspoon red pepper flakes

Pasta Ingredients

- 1 1lb. bag (16 ounces) of your favorite pasta, any shape
- 2 teaspoons salt
- 1 cup Green Goddess Dressing (see page 181)

How To Prep The Pasta

1. Bring a large pot to a boil. Add 2 teaspoons of salt into the water for seasoning. Once the water is boiling, add your pasta and stir to cook.
2. Cook it 1 minute shy of the package directions. Drain and add it back into the pot.
3. Pour the container of green goddess dressing into the pot with the pasta and stir well.

INSTRUCTIONS

How To Cook The Shrimp

1. Shrimp should be defrosted gradually in the refrigerator overnight or quickly by keeping it in the bag and running under cold running water for about 15-20 minutes to ensure they stay firm and safe to eat.
2. Into a bowl, add olive oil, garlic powder, salt, pepper and paprika. Mix well.
3. Add the shrimp to the bowl with the seasonings and mix to coat.
4. Place shrimp onto an air fryer baking tray in an even layer.
5. Air fry at 400F for 8 minutes until the shrimp is pink. Internal temperature should reach 145F.
6. Serve the shrimp with the green goddess pasta. Enjoy!

EASY TORTELLINI PASTA SALAD

Yield: 4 Servings | Total Time: 16 Min

When I know we are going to have a busy week, I prep this big pasta salad. It stays in the fridge well, and frankly gets better over time. We enjoy it as a quick lunch, small snack or on the go in a container! I love it because it doesn't require a microwave!

INGREDIENTS

- 1 16 oz package of cheese tortellini
- 1 teaspoon salt
- 1 small red onion, diced
- 2 bell peppers, diced
- 4 Persian cucumbers, diced
- 10 slices of salami or any deli meat, thinly sliced
- 1/3 cup Pecorino Romano blend

Dressing

- 1/4 cup red wine vinegar
- 1/4 cup olive oil
- 1/4 teaspoon salt
- 1/4 teaspoon pepper
- 1/4 teaspoon garlic powder

INSTRUCTIONS

1. Heat a pot with water and salt over high heat to boil. Cook the tortellini according to package directions (about 4-6 mins). Drain & set aside.

2. Prep the rest of the ingredients and add them to a bowl along with the cooked tortellini.

3. Shake the dressing in a mason jar & add it to the pasta salad.

4. Serve this cold or warm.

   SUBSTITUTIONS

   Use any tortellini available to you, this can be meatless or with meat.

5. Swap salami for oven-roasted turkey breast or chicken breast. If you want it meatless, omit the deli meat and add canned chickpeas.

TRADER JOE'S LENTIL BRUSCHETTA FLATBREAD

Yield: 4 | Total Time: 30 Min

My mom taught me this recipe over 10 years ago and we make it at least once a month. It is so scary how easy it is, and everyone always loves it. It's a great option for vegetarian families!

INGREDIENTS

- 1 pack Trader Joe's steamed lentils
- 1 14 oz container of Trader Joe's bruschetta
- 2 teaspoons oregano, dried
- 4 pieces Trader Joe's whole-wheat flatbread (or other store-bought whole-wheat flatbread)
- 1 cup shredded mozzarella cheese
- fresh basil leaves, for garnish

INSTRUCTIONS

1. Preheat the oven to 400F or, if you are just making one pizza, preheat the air fryer to 400F.

2. Mix the steamed lentils, bruschetta, and oregano in a large bowl.

3. Depending on the size of your flatbread, add about 1/4 cup - 1/2 cup of the mixture on each tortilla. Spread it evenly, careful not to spread it too far onto the edges. You want to make sure it's not on too thick either as it won't allow the flatbread to crisp up.

4. Sprinkle the flatbread with the shredded cheese, as much or as little as you want. Again, careful not to overfill the flatbread.

5. Place the flatbreads on a baking sheet and bake for about 12-15 minutes. Keep an eye on them t make sure the cheese gets golden brown, but doesn't burn.

6. If you are using an air fryer, check it after 10 minutes to see how to cheese is melting.

7. Finish with a sprinkle of fresh chopped basil on top.

8. Cut with a pizza cutter and enjoy warm!

Jazz's Tricks

Storage: If there is additional filling leftover, you can store this in the fridge for up to 4 days.

Use the extra filling the next night on a bed of arugula, brown rice, toasted bread or your favorite pasta!

Use whole-wheat or regular flatbread or naan.

BBQ CHICKEN PIZZA

Yield: 2 Pizzas | Total Time: 25 Min

INGREDIENTS

- 2 whole-wheat tortillas
- 1 cup shredded chicken breast
- 1/2 cup BBQ sauce (divided into 1/4 cup portions)
- 1/2 cup shredded cheddar cheese
- 1/4 cup thinly sliced red onion
- 1/4 cup freshly chopped cilantro

INSTRUCTIONS

1. Preheat your oven to 425°F (220°C).

2. Place the whole-wheat tortillas on a baking sheet.

3. Spread 1/4 cup of BBQ sauce evenly over each tortilla. Be careful not to use too much sauce to avoid sogginess.

4. Sprinkle the shredded cheddar cheese evenly on top of the BBQ sauce.

5. In a small bowl, mix the shredded chicken with the remaining 1/4 cup of BBQ sauce until the chicken is well coated.

6. Spread the BBQ chicken mixture evenly over the tortillas.

7. Top with the thinly sliced red onions.

8. Bake the pizzas in the preheated oven for about 15 minutes, or until the tortillas are golden brown and crispy.

9. Remove the pizzas from the oven and sprinkle with the freshly chopped cilantro.

10. Cut each pizza into 4 triangles using a pizza cutter or a sharp knife.

Jazz's Tricks

- Use a rotisserie chicken for ease!
- Use any pizza crust you prefer. Naan and pita work well!

VEGAN GLUTEN-FREE MAC N CHEESE RECIPE

Yield: 4-6 Servings | Total Time: 35 Min

Most Mac & Cheese recipes are filled with cream, butter and cheese. I created this recipe when I was eating dairy-free and I wanted to bring something to our family Thanksgiving! Everyone was surprised there was no dairy in it! I always make it for any vegan friends!

INGREDIENTS

Cheese Sauce

- 1 cup raw cashews
- 1 teaspoon salt
- 1 teaspoon garlic powder
- 1/4 teaspoon turmeric
- 1 teaspoon mustard
- 1/2 lemon, juiced
- 1/4 cup nutritional yeast
- 1 cup starchy pasta cooking water

Pasta Ingredients

- 8-10 oz of gluten-free pasta, I used shells
- 2 teaspoons salt (for pasta water)

Breadcrumb Topping

- 1 cup gluten-free breadcrumbs
- 1 tablespoon olive oil
- 1 teaspoon salt

INSTRUCTIONS

1. Preheat the oven to 375F.

2. Soak raw cashews in boiling water for 5 mins. Then drain.

3. Salt a stockpot of water and cook the pasta according to package directions (subtract 2 minutes for al dente). While the pasta is cooking, use a mug to reserve 1 cup of starchy pasta cooking water. This will be used to add to the cheese sauce! Drain the water and put the cooked pasta back in the stockpot.

4. In a blender, make the cheese sauce. Add the drained cashews, salt, garlic powder, turmeric, mustard, lemon juice, nutritional yeast and starchy pasta cooking water. Blend the cheese sauce in a high-powered blender.

5. Once the sauce is smooth, add the sauce to the cooked pasta!

6. In a bowl, make the breadcrumb topping by mixing together breadcrumbs, olive oil and salt.

7. Transfer the pasta with cheese sauce into an oven-safe baking dish, top with the breadcrumb topping evenly.

8. Bake at 375F for 15-20 minutes until the breadcrumbs are toasted and golden brown!

9. Let it sit for 10 minutes before digging in.

10. Enjoy!

PESTO GNOCCHI BOWL

Yield: 2 Servings | Total Time: 20 Min

INGREDIENTS

- 16 oz package of gnocchi
- Olive oil or avocado oil spray
- 1 can of chickpeas, drained and rinsed
- 1/2 cup frozen spinach
- 1/3 cup jarred pesto
- 2 tablespoons sun-dried tomatoes
- 1/2 lemon, juiced (about 1-2 tablespoons)
- 1/2 teaspoon sea salt
- Fresh basil leaves for garnish

INSTRUCTIONS

1. Preheat your air fryer to 400°F (200°C).
2. Spray the air fryer basket with cooking spray. Add the gnocchi to the oiled air fryer basket. Air fry for 15 minutes, shaking halfway through, until golden brown and crispy.
3. While the gnocchi is cooking, prepare the rest of the ingredients. Warm the frozen spinach in the microwave for 30 seconds to thaw and chop the sun-dried tomatoes.
4. Add the drained chickpeas, spinach, pesto, chopped sun-dried tomatoes into a large mixing bowl.
5. Once the gnocchi is done, add it to the bowl.
6. Finish with the pesto, lemon juice and sea salt. Mix everything together thoroughly.
7. Finish with fresh basil leaves on top.

Jazz's Tricks

1. You can swap the gnocchi for cauliflower gnocchi. Cooking instructions remain the same.
2. Use a vegan pesto if you prefer this to be dairy-free.
3. If you don't have an air fryer, you can make the gnocchi in the oven. Cook in a preheated oven at 425°F (220°C) for 20-25 minutes, flipping halfway through.

BUTTERNUT SQUASH RAVIOLI WITH SAGE BUTTER SAUCE

Yield: 2 Servings | Total Time: 10 Min

Ravioli has to be my favorite food, but when it's paired with this brown butter sauce, it feels like it was made in a restaurant. I make this when I feel like I need a comfort meal.

INGREDIENTS

- 9 oz (1 pack) of butternut squash ravioli
- 4 tablespoons of butter
- 10 fresh sage leaves, chopped
- 1/2 teaspoon salt
- 1/2 teaspoon pepper
- 1/4 teaspoon red pepper flakes
- 1/2 cup grated Pecorino Romano

INSTRUCTIONS

1. Bring a pot of water to a boil for the ravioli. Salt the water and bring it to a boil. Once it comes to a boil, carefully drop your ravioli into the pasta water. Cook for about 4 minutes (this will depend on your package instructions). Careful not to overcook. While the pasta is cooking, reserve about 1/4 cup of the pasta water in a coffee mug and set aside. Drain the ravioli.

2. Cube the butter into smaller pieces and add it into a larger skillet over medium heat, stirring occasionally. Stir the butter continuously until small bubbles begin to foam and a slightly nutty aroma arises. This is the butter browning! Watch the butter carefully to make sure it doesn't burn. This will take about 4 minutes.

3. Chop the sage into smaller pieces. Once the butter browns, turn the heat to low and add the sage pieces to slightly crisp for 1 minute.

4. Add the cooked ravioli along with 2 tablespoons of the starchy pasta water you reserved. Toss to coat.

5. Finish with a sprinkle of salt, pepper and red pepper flakes.

6. To plate, serve with a Pecorino Romano sprinkle on top for added creaminess and flavor. Add any excess brown butter on top.

MINI AIR FRYER PIZZA

Yield: 6 Mini Pizzas | Total time: 20 Min

INGREDIENTS

- 1 12-oz package store-bought pizza dough
- 1 tablespoon olive oil
- 3/4 teaspoon garlic powder
- 1 cup marinara sauce
- 1 cup mozzarella pearls
- 1 12-oz package turkey pepperoni slices (about 3/4 cup)
- Fresh basil leaves
- 1/2 cup grated Parmesan cheese
- Flour (for dusting)

INSTRUCTIONS

1. Lightly dust your working surface with flour.

2. Cut the dough into smaller, manageable sections (about 6 parts).

3. Roll each section into a ball with your hands, then flatten and roll out to about 1/4 inch thickness using a rolling pin to make about 3-4 inches in diameter.

4. Preheat your air fryer to 400°F for about 3-5 minutes.

5. Place parchment paper on the bottom of your air fryer, and place the flattened dough in the air fryer. Make sure not to overlap the pizzas, you may need to work in batches.

6. Start with spreading a drizzle of olive oil, and a sprinkle of garlic powder on each one.

7. Air fry the dough rounds at 350°F for about 3-4 minutes, or until they start to puff up and slightly firm.

8. Keep the pizza dough in the air fryer, and add your toppings right there.

9. Spread a spoonful of marinara sauce, a few mozzarella pearls, turkey pepperoni and parmesan cheese on top.

10. Air fry at 350°F for another 4-5 minutes, or until the crust is golden and the cheese is melted and bubbly.

11. Once cooked, remove the mini pizzas carefully from the air fryer using a spatula. Top with fresh basil leaves.

Jazz's Tricks

- Use parchment paper in the air fryer to make sure the pizza dough doesn't stick. Alternatively, you can spray the air fryer with olive oil.
- Assemble the pizzas in the air fryer, it's easier than transporting them in and out of the air fryer.
- Remove the pizzas from the air fryer basket with a spatula, not tongs to make sure the toppings stay intact!

CREAMY COTTAGE CHEESE PASTA

Yield: 4 Servings | Total Time: 35 Min

INGREDIENTS

Sauce

- 2 tablespoons olive oil
- 1 medium yellow onion, diced
- 5 cloves garlic, minced
- 1 15-oz can diced tomatoes
- 3 tablespoons lemon juice
- 1/2 teaspoon pepper
- 1/4 teaspoon salt
- 1 cup cottage cheese
- 1/2 cup pasta water
- 1/2 cup shredded parmesan cheese

Pasta

- 1 lb pasta, I used fusilli
- 1 teaspoon salt
- Fresh basil, for serving

INSTRUCTIONS

1. To cook the pasta, fill a large stockpot with water and 1 teaspoon of salt. Heat on high until the water boils.
2. Add the pasta and cook according to the package directions. Reserve 1/2 cup of pasta water, then drain the pasta and set aside.
3. To prepare the sauce, heat the olive oil in a large saucepan over medium-low heat.
4. Add the diced onion. Sauté for about 7 minutes until the onions are translucent. Add the minced garlic. Cook for 30 seconds to 1 minute, stirring occasionally.
5. Stir in the diced tomatoes, lemon juice, salt, and pepper. Simmer on medium heat for about 10 minutes, stirring occasionally.
6. Transfer the cooked tomato mixture to a blender. Add the cottage cheese and the 1/2 cup of reserved pasta water.
7. Blend until the mixture is smooth. Make sure the steam can escape from the blender while blending.
8. Pour the creamy sauce back into the saucepan. Add the cooked pasta and shredded parmesan cheese.
9. Stir well to combine all the ingredients.
10. Serve the pasta hot, with fresh basil.

Jazz's Tricks

- You can use any pasta you prefer! I love using penne and rigatoni too. You can also use whole wheat, brown rice or any other pasta alternatives!
- If you want a bit of spice, add red pepper flakes to the tomato sauce!
- Store any leftovers in an airtight container in the fridge for up to 3 days.

LEMON-CAPER CHICKEN PICCATA

Yield: 4 Servings | Total Time: 30 Min

INGREDIENTS

- 2 lbs chicken breasts
- 1 teaspoon salt, divided
- 1/2 teaspoon pepper
- 1/4 cup arrowroot flour
- 2 tablespoons avocado oil
- 1 tablespoon butter
- 3 cloves garlic, minced
- 2 tablespoons capers, drained
- 1 cup chicken broth
- 2 lemons, juiced
- 1 tablespoon fresh parsley, chopped
- 1 pack of your favorite gluten-free noodles
- 1 teaspoon salt (for pasta water)

INSTRUCTIONS

1. Bring a large pot of water to a boil. Add 1 teaspoon salt to the water.

2. Cook the gluten-free noodles according to the package instructions until al dente. Drain and set aside.

3. Slice the chicken breasts into thin cutlets. Season both sides of the chicken with 1/2 teaspoon salt and 1/2 teaspoon pepper.

4. Pour the arrowroot flour onto a large plate. Dredge each chicken cutlet in the flour, shaking off any excess. Set aside.

5. Heat a large skillet over medium-high heat. Once the skillet is warm, add 2 tablespoons of avocado oil.

6. Once the oil is hot, add the chicken cutlets to the skillet, being careful not to overcrowd the pan. Cook the chicken for about 3-4 minutes per side, or until golden brown and cooked through. If necessary, work in batches.

7. Remove the cooked chicken from the skillet and place it on a clean plate.

8. In the same skillet, reduce the heat to low and add 1 tablespoon butter. Allow it to melt.

9. Add the minced garlic to the skillet and stir for 30 seconds, until fragrant.

10. Stir in the capers, chicken broth, and juice of 2 lemons. Mix well and let it simmer for a few minutes to combine the flavors.

11. Return the cooked chicken to the skillet, nestling it into the sauce. Let the chicken simmer in the sauce for about 5 minutes, so it absorbs the flavors and becomes tender.

12. Plate the cooked pasta and top with the chicken cutlets and the warm piccata sauce. Garnish with chopped fresh parsley.

Jazz's Tricks

- Store any leftovers in an airtight container in the refrigerator for up to 3 days. Reheat gently on the stove to avoid overcooking the chicken.

HEARTY BOLOGNESE SKILLET

Yield: 4 Servings | Total Time: 40 Min

INGREDIENTS

- 2 tablespoons olive oil
- 1 onion, finely diced
- 2 celery stalks, finely diced
- 2 carrots, finely diced
- 3 cloves garlic, minced
- 2 tablespoons tomato paste
- 1 lb ground turkey
- 1 jar (24 oz) marinara pasta sauce
- ½ teaspoon salt (more or less to taste)
- ½ teaspoon pepper (more or less to taste)
- 1lb pasta (16 ounces)
- 1 teaspoon salt (for pasta)
- Grated parmesan cheese (optional, for serving)

INSTRUCTIONS

1. Heat 1 tablespoon of olive oil in a large skillet or saucepan over medium heat.
2. Add the diced onion, celery, and carrots. Sauté for about 5-7 minutes, stirring occasionally, until the vegetables are softened and slightly caramelized.
3. Add the minced garlic to the skillet. Cook for 1 minute, stirring, until the garlic becomes fragrant.
4. Push the vegetables to one side of the skillet. Add the ground turkey to the empty side of the skillet.
5. Break up the turkey with a spatula and cook for 5-7 minutes, or until it is no longer pink.
6. Mix the cooked turkey with the softened vegetables.
7. Make a small space in the center of the skillet and add the tomato paste. Stir it for 1 minute until it heats up, then mix it into the turkey and vegetables.
8. Pour the jar of pasta sauce into the skillet. Stir well to combine all ingredients.
9. Reduce the heat to low and let the sauce simmer for 15-20 minutes, stirring occasionally. This helps the flavors meld together and the sauce to thicken slightly.
10. Taste the sauce and add salt and pepper as needed.
11. Meanwhile, cook your pasta according to the package instructions until al dente. Drain the pasta.
12. Add the cooked pasta to the skillet with the turkey bolognese sauce. Toss everything together until the pasta is well coated with the sauce.
13. Serve hot with grated parmesan cheese on top if desired.

Jazz's Tricks

- Make sure to dice the vegetables finely so they blend well into the sauce.
- Store leftovers in an airtight container in the refrigerator for up to 4 days. Reheat gently on the stove or in the microwave.
- The sauce can be frozen for up to 3 months. Thaw and reheat before serving.

Vegetarian

Go-to meatless meals

I love incorporating meatless meals into my routine, and these are my favorite go-to recipes. They're designed to keep you full and satisfied, without feeling like you're missing out on anything. Whether you're cutting back on meat or don't eat it at all, these dishes are here to make meatless eating both enjoyable and satisfying.

VEGAN BLACK BEAN TOSTADA

Yield: 2 Servings | Total Time: 20 Min

INGREDIENTS

- 4 corn tortillas
- 1 teaspoon avocado oil
- ⅛ teaspoon salt
- 1 can (15 oz) black beans, drained and rinsed
- 2 limes, juiced
- 1 teaspoon Tajín or Chili Lime seasoning, divided into ½ teaspoons
- 1 avocado, sliced
- ¼ cup whole kernel corn
- ¼ cup green onion, chopped
- ¼ cup tomato, chopped

INSTRUCTIONS

1. Preheat your oven to 400°F (200°C).

2. Brush both sides of the corn tortillas with avocado oil evenly. Arrange the tortillas on a baking sheet, making sure they don't overlap. Sprinkle a little bit of salt on top.

3. Bake for 10 minutes, flipping them halfway through (5 minutes on each side) until they are crisp. Alternatively, you can do this step in an air fryer. Air fry at 400°F (200°C) for about 5 minutes, flipping halfway through.

4. In a bowl, combine the black beans, lime juice, and 1/2 teaspoon of Tajín. Mash with a fork until you achieve a spreadable consistency.

5. Remove the tortillas from the oven and let them cool for about 5 minutes.

6. Assemble the tostadas by spreading a layer of the mashed black beans on each tortilla. Add the corn, tomatoes, avocado slices, and green onion on top. Sprinkle with the remaining Tajín seasoning.

QUICK & EASY GAME DAY VEGETARIAN CHILI

Yield: 6-8 servings | Total time: 25 minutes

INGREDIENTS

- 2 cups of vegetable broth (or chicken broth if you prefer and are not vegetarian)
- 1 (15-oz) can of kidney beans
- 1 (15-oz) can of black beans
- 1 (15-oz) can of garbanzo beans
- 1 (16-oz) jar of salsa
- 1 cup of uncooked pasta
- 1 cup of Mexican cheese
- 1 red onion, diced
- 1 teaspoon garlic, minced
- 2 limes, juiced
- 1 teaspoon avocado oil
- 1 tablespoon paprika
- 1 tablespoon dried parsley
- 1 tablespoon dried basil
- 1 teaspoon dried oregano
- 1-2 teaspoons chili powder
- 1/2 teaspoon pink salt
- 1/2 teaspoon pepper

INSTRUCTIONS

1. In a large stockpot, heat the avocado oil over medium heat. Add the chopped onion and garlic, and cook for 5-8 minutes until the onion is translucent.

2. While the onion and garlic are cooking, drain and rinse the kidney beans, black beans, and garbanzo beans.

3. Add the drained beans, salsa, vegetable broth, lime juice, and spices to the stockpot. Stir gently to combine, being careful not to mash the beans.

4. Add the dry pasta noodles to the stockpot. Stir to make sure the noodles are fully covered by the broth. Let the mixture simmer on medium-low heat for about 15 minutes, stirring occasionally, until the noodles are cooked.

5. Remove the stockpot from heat, stir in the cheese until it's melted, and serve the chili warm.

STORAGE:

Store any leftovers in an airtight container in the fridge for up to 3-4 days.

EASY VEGAN BLACK BEAN AIR FRYER TACOS

Yield: 4-6 Servings | Total Time: 20 Min

I make these for taco night because they are so easy. I make them ahead of time and pop them in the air fryer. Everyone loves customizing the toppings so I usually set out some cilantro, salsa and guacamole for topping!

INGREDIENTS

- 12-14 tortillas
- 1 15-oz can black beans
- 4 garlic cloves
- 1 chipotle in adobo sauce, optional
- 1 teaspoon cumin
- 1 teaspoon chili powder
- ½ teaspoon salt
- 1/2 teaspoon pepper
- ¼ teaspoon cayenne pepper
- ½ cup shredded vegan cheese
- 1 cup shredded lettuce
- 1 cup pico de gallo
- 1/4 cup guacamole
- 1 lime, cut into wedges for serving

INSTRUCTIONS

1. Open the can of black beans. Rinse them and drain them off the water.
2. Add the black beans into your food processor along with the cloves of garlic, chipotle, cumin, chili powder, salt, pepper, and cayenne pepper. Pulse the ingredients together in the food processor until it is smooth. You may need to use a rubber spatula to scrape down the sides.
3. Lay your tortillas flat and scoop about 2 tablespoons of the black bean mixture evenly into each tortilla.
4. Add a sprinkle of cheese on top of the black bean spread. You can add as much or as little cheese as desired. About 1 tablespoon is a great place to start.
5. Fold each tortilla over, and continue until all of your tortillas are filled.
6. Spray both sides of the tacos with olive oil spray, or use a paper towel to rub olive oil on the outside.
7. Place them in the air fryer in a single even layer, careful not to overlap. You may need to work in batches.
8. Air fry at 400F for 8-10 minutes until the tortillas are golden brown. Flip them half way through to cook evenly on both sides.
9. Once they are done cooking, remove from the air fryer, open them up and stuff with shredded lettuce and pico de gallo.
10. Serve with guacamole for dipping and lime wedges on top!

COCONUT CHICKPEA CURRY

Yield: 4 servings | Total Time: 30 Min

I crave this every single winter. Anytime anyone is sick or if the weather is cold outside, this is my go-to. My dad doesn't like curry but even he loved this recipe! It's unique and truly one of my favorite comfort dishes!

INGREDIENTS

Curry

- 3 cups spinach, fresh
- 1 (15.5 oz) can chickpeas
- 1 (13.5 oz) can full-fat coconut milk
- 1 cup onion, diced (about 1 small onion)
- 2 tablespoons lime juice
- 1 tablespoon coconut oil
- 1 tablespoon curry powder
- 2 teaspoons salt
- 1 teaspoon garlic powder
- 1/2 teaspoon turmeric
- 1/8 teaspoon black pepper

Rice

- 2 cups Basmati rice
- 2 3/4 cup water
- 1 teaspoon salt

INSTRUCTIONS

1. Wash the rice. Place rice in a saucepan and cover the rice with water. Swirl your hands through the water, then drain carefully. Repeat about 5-6 times until the water being drained is no longer cloudy.

2. In the same saucepan, add the water and salt to the rice. Bring rice to a boil (about 3-4 minutes) then cover with a lid and reduce heat to medium-low for about 15 minutes.

3. To cook the curry, heat the coconut oil in a large pan on medium-high.

4. Add the onion into the warm oil and sauté for about 5 minutes until translucent.

5. While the onion is cooking, drain and rinse the canned chickpeas. Set aside.

6. Add curry powder, salt, garlic powder, turmeric and black pepper to the onion and sauté for about 30 seconds until fragrant.

7. Add the chickpeas and coconut milk to the pan. Mix to combine. Cover with a lid, reduce heat to low, and simmer for 10 minutes, stirring occasionally.

8. Remove curry from heat. Add fresh chopped spinach, stirring until wilted and warm. Add the lime juice. Stir to combine.

9. Serve curry over the fluffy white rice.

GLUTEN-FREE AND DAIRY-FREE CAULIFLOWER RISOTTO

Yield: 4 servings | Total Time: 30 Min

I made this for my mom over 10 years ago and she still brings it up from time to time. She always asks me to make it for her every time I am with her.

INGREDIENTS

- 1 tablespoon avocado oil
- 1/2 onion, diced
- 3 cloves garlic, minced
- 8 oz sliced mushrooms
- 1/2 cup vegetable stock or chicken stock, if you are not vegan
- 12 oz riced cauliflower, frozen or fresh
- 2 tablespoons sun-dried tomato or 1 tablespoon of lemon juice
- 1 teaspoon salt
- 1/2 teaspoon oregano
- 1/4 teaspoon pepper
- 1/2 cup fresh parsley, chopped
- 1/2 cup your favorite cheese, plant-based works too

INSTRUCTIONS

1. Heat a non-stick skillet on medium heat with 1 tablespoon of avocado oil.
2. Once the oil is heated, add the onion and sauté for 5 minutes. Add the garlic and sauté for 30 seconds. Add the mushrooms, cauliflower rice, and seasonings and continue cooking for another 5 minutes.
3. Add vegetable broth and cover and simmer for 10 minutes on medium/low heat.
4. Finally, add the sun-dried tomatoes or lemon juice, seasonings, cheese and parsley. Stir to combine until cheese is melted.
5. Enjoy within 4 days!

THE BEST AIR FRYER EGGPLANT PARMESAN

Yield: 2 servings | Total time: 33 Min

Traditional eggplant parmesan was always hard to make with the copious amount of steps. I created a shortcut for the nights we are craving eggplant parm, this is it! Around 30 minutes and it's done!

INGREDIENTS

- 1 eggplant
- 1/2 teaspoon salt (for drying eggplant)
- 2 tablespoons olive oil
- ¼ teaspoon salt
- ¼ teaspoon pepper
- 1 cup marinara sauce
- 1 tablespoon Italian seasoning
- 1 cup shredded mozzarella
- 2 tablespoons parmesan cheese
- 1 tablespoon chopped basil

INSTRUCTIONS

1. Start by washing the eggplant and cutting off the stem end. Then, halve the eggplant lengthwise to create two equal halves.

2. Score the flesh of the eggplant, making sure to not cut through the skin. Score the eggplant the other direction, creating a cross-hatch. Gently turn the eggplant inside out to open up the eggplant.

3. Sprinkle salt on the eggplant and let it set aside for 10 minutes to remove the liquid. Dab with a paper towel to remove the excess liquid.

4. Preheat the air fryer to 375°F (190°C) for a few minutes according to the manufacturer's instructions.

5. Once dry, brush the cut side of each eggplant half with olive oil and sprinkle with a pinch of salt and black pepper.

6. Place the eggplant halves, cut side up, in the air fryer basket. Cook for about 15 minutes at 375°F (190°C) until the eggplant is tender.

7. Remove the basket from the air fryer and spread 1/2 cup of marinara sauce over the cut side of each eggplant half. Then sprinkle with the Italian seasoning for flavor.

8. Sprinkle 1/2 cup shredded mozzarella cheese and 1 tablespoon parmesan cheese over each eggplant half evenly.

9. Return the basket to the air fryer and cook for an additional 7 minutes, or until the cheese is melted and bubbly.

10. Remove the eggplant halves from the air fryer and garnish with chopped fresh basil. Let the eggplant cool slightly before serving.

VEGAN CHICKPEA BURGER RECIPE

Yield: 6 | Total Time: 33 Min

I made these burgers every time I catered for a wellness retreat. Everyone loved the freshness of them. I usually served it with traditional burger toppings but it's also great on salads! They freeze well too!

INGREDIENTS

- 1 teaspoon avocado oil
- 1 onion, diced
- 3 cloves garlic, minced
- 1 can chickpeas, drained and rinsed
- 1/2 teaspoon paprika
- 1/2 teaspoon coriander
- 1/2 teaspoon cumin
- 1/2 cup chopped cilantro
- 1/2 cup flour (gluten-free, whole-wheat, white or oat works), divided
- 2 tablespoons avocado oil

INSTRUCTIONS

1. Dice the onion and mince your garlic.

2. Heat a skillet to medium heat. Add the avocado oil. Once it's hot (30 seconds or so), then add the diced onion and minced garlic. Sauté until the onions are translucent (about 5 minutes). Careful not to burn the garlic.

3. Drain the can of chickpeas and rinse it to remove any excess coating. Add the drained and rinsed chickpeas to a food processor. Pulse a few times.

4. Add the sautéed onion and garlic directly to the food processor. Add your spices like paprika, coriander, cumin, fresh cilantro and ¼ cup of flour directly into the food processor.

5. Blend for 30 seconds (scraping down the sides if necessary) until well combined. Add the remaining 1/4 cup flour, process again.

6. Sprinkle 1 tablespoon of flour onto the counter and roll the dough into 6 even rounds. I like using an ice cream scoop or cookie scooper to get even shapes.

7. Place the burger patties on a parchment paper-lined baking sheet, pressing down with the back of a cup to flatten slightly.

8. Place the baking sheet in the freezer for about 20 minutes to firm the veggie patties.

9. After 20 minutes, heat a skillet over medium heat with 2 tablespoons avocado oil. Once hot, add the burgers to the oil & shallow fry for 5 minutes each side.

10. Serve however you like! I love using them on a big salad, over rice with veggies, with my favorite bun & burger toppings or just as a simple handheld snack.

BRIE CAPRESE PASTA

Yield: 4 Servings | Total Time: 30 Min

INGREDIENTS

- 10 oz spaghetti
- 1 teaspoon salt (for pasta water)
- 2 tablespoons butter
- 1 white onion, diced
- 4 cloves garlic, minced
- 1 pint cherry or grape tomatoes, cut in half
- 1/2 teaspoon salt
- 1/2 teaspoon oregano
- 1/4 teaspoon pepper
- 1/4 teaspoon red pepper flakes (adjust based on taste preferences)
- 1 cup brie cheese, cut into cubes
- 1 cup fresh basil
- 1 teaspoon balsamic vinegar
- 1 teaspoon balsamic glaze

INSTRUCTIONS

1. Fill a large pot with water and add about 1 teaspoon of salt.

2. Bring the water to a boil, then add the spaghetti.

3. Cook the pasta according to the package directions, but make sure to stop cooking just before it is fully done (al dente). This means the pasta should still have a slight firmness when you bite into it.

4. Before draining the pasta, scoop out 1/2 cup of the cooking water with a mug and set it aside. This starchy water will help make your sauce become creamy.

5. In a large skillet, melt the butter over medium heat.

6. Once the butter is warmed, add the diced onion and garlic and cook for about 4 minutes, until the onions become soft and translucent.

7. Add the tomatoes, oregano, salt, pepper, and red pepper flakes to the skillet and cook for another 4 minutes, until the tomatoes start to soften.

8. Add the cubes of brie cheese and the reserved pasta water to the skillet. Stir gently until the cheese melts and blends into the sauce.

9. Add the cooked pasta to the skillet and toss everything together until the pasta is well-coated with the sauce.

10. Drizzle the spaghetti with balsamic vinegar, fresh basil, and balsamic glaze.

11. Taste and adjust seasonings if needed. Serve immediately and enjoy.

QUICK AND EASY LEMONY QUINOA

Yield: 4 Servings | Total Time: 30 Min

If I have time on Sundays, I will always make a batch of this quinoa. It's versatile enough for salads, breakfast bowls, and as a rice substitute. It's packed with protein too!

INGREDIENTS

- 1 cup quinoa
- 2 cups chicken broth
- 1 tablespoon lemon zest
- 2 tablespoons lemon juice
- 1/4 teaspoon salt or to taste

INSTRUCTIONS

1. Rinse your quinoa under cold water using a fine-mesh strainer.

2. Combine the rinsed quinoa, chicken broth and salt into a saucepan. Turn the heat on high and bring it to a boil.

3. Once the mixture comes to a boil, reduce the heat to low and put the top on the saucepan for about 10 minutes until the quinoa is fluffy.

4. Once fluffy, turn off the heat, add in the lemon juice and zest. Mix to combine well.

5. Enjoy it as a side dish, as a base for stews, as a rice substitution or add it into salads!

FLUFFY BASMATI RICE

Yield: 4 Servings | Total Time: 25 Min

Growing up my mom made this rice recipe almost every single night. It's now my comfort in a bowl. Some nights I just have this with plain yogurt and it's my favorite dinner!

INGREDIENTS

- 2 cups long grain basmati rice
- 4 cups water
- 1 teaspoon salt
- 1 teaspoon avocado oil or olive oil

INSTRUCTIONS

1. Place the basmati rice in a stockpot and rinse it under cold water for about 6-8 times, or until the water runs clear. Add 4 cups of cold water to the rinsed rice. Then, add the salt and avocado oil, mixing to combine.

2. Place the stockpot on the stove over medium-high heat and allow it to come to a boil. Once the rice is boiling, reduce the heat to low and cover the pot with a lid. Let the rice simmer for 10 minutes.

3. After 10 minutes, remove the pot from the heat. Fluff the rice with a fork before serving to achieve a light and fluffy texture. Enjoy your fluffy basmati rice as a perfect side dish or base for your favorite meals!

AIR FRYER MAC AND CHEESE

Yield: 2 Servings | Total Time: 35 Min

This is my favorite mac & cheese method because it has very minimal cleanup, there is no need to boil noodles and the texture turns out extra creamy! This is one of those recipes that gets even better by sitting in the fridge. It's crazy how easy it is!

INGREDIENTS

- 1 ½ cups dried shells
- 1 ½ cups whole milk
- 2 cups shredded sharp cheddar cheese
- 2 tablespoon unsalted butter
- 3/4 teaspoon dry mustard powder
- ¼ teaspoon grated nutmeg
- ¼ teaspoon garlic powder
- ¼ teaspoon black pepper
- ¼ cup parmesan cheese

INSTRUCTIONS

1. Preheat the air fryer to 360°F for 10 minutes.

2. Mix the pasta, milk, cheddar cheese, butter, mustard powder, nutmeg, garlic powder, and pepper in a large oven-safe dish that fits in your air fryer.

3. Spray an air fryer baking dish with cooking spray, then pour the mac and cheese mixture into the dish.

4. Air fry for 22 minutes, stirring every 5 minutes to mix the ingredients well.

5. In the last 2 minutes, top with parmesan cheese. Continue air frying until the top is golden brown (about 2 minutes).

6. Rest the dish for 5-7 minutes to let it thicken and get creamy. Enjoy!

Chicken,Beef & Turkey

Effortless, Flavorful Recipes forEvery Cook

This section is all about unique and flavorful chicken and beef dishes that won't keep you in the kitchen for hours. Designed with beginner cooks in mind, these recipes are straightforward and satisfying. Whether you're looking for a quick weeknight dinner or something a bit more special, these meals are perfect for anyone wanting delicious results without the fuss.

CRISPY AIR FRYER BUFFALO CHICKEN TENDERS

Yield: 2 - 4 servings | Total Time: 30 Min

This is so easy my husband can make it! He loves having a big batch of these made in the fridge. One day he will have it with carrots and celery, the next day he will have it on a big salad or with fries. It's easy to prep!

INGREDIENTS

- 1 lb chicken tenders
- 1/3 cup buffalo wing sauce
- 1 tablespoon mayonnaise
- 1 teaspoon paprika
- 1 teaspoon garlic powder
- 1 teaspoon onion powder
- 1/2 teaspoon salt
- 1/2 teaspoon black pepper
- Parsley for garnish (optional)

INSTRUCTIONS

1. Add the buffalo sauce, mayonnaise, paprika, garlic powder, onion powder, salt, and pepper to a large bowl.

2. Mix it together until it is mostly smooth.

3. Add your chicken tenders into the bowl and mix to coat. Let this sit for anywhere from 10 minutes up to 24 hours. If you plan to marinate for more than 15 minutes, pop them into an airtight container in the fridge. Otherwise, keep them on the counter.

4. Preheat your air fryer at 375 F for 4 minutes.

5. Spray your air fryer basket with cooking spray. I like to use avocado oil.

6. Place the marinated chicken tenders into a single layer in your air fryer basket. Make sure the tenders are not touching each other in the basket, this will allow for even cooking.

7. Air fry at 375 F for 12 minutes, flipping halfway. They are ready when the internal temperature reaches at least 165F.

8. Remove from the air fryer and let them cool before enjoying!

9. Finish with a sprinkle of parsley and serve alongside your favorite dipping sauce!

3-INGREDIENT AIR FRYER CHICKEN NUGGETS

Yield: 22 Nuggets | Total Time: 25 Min

I stopped buying store-bought chicken nuggets because it was hard to find one with decent ingredients. I just make my own and it tastes so juicy on the inside and crispy on the outside. Bonus is that it only calls for 3 ingredients!

INGREDIENTS

- 1 lb chicken, cut into bite-sized nuggets
- 2 large eggs
- 5 oz BBQ potato chips
- Optional: avocado oil spray

INSTRUCTIONS

1. Preheat your air fryer to 400F.

2. Pop the BBQ potato chips into a food processor and pulse for 10 seconds until it forms into crumbs. Alternatively, you can also put the chips into a large Ziploc bag and roll with a rolling pin. Place them in a bowl.

3. Crack the eggs into another small bowl. Whisk with a fork.

4. To begin assembly of the chicken nuggets, dip each chicken piece into the whisked eggs, then the crumbled potato chips. Ensure even coating on all sides. You may want to press the crumbs on the chicken to make sure it adheres to the chicken bites.

5. Arrange each chicken nugget in the air fryer basket, making sure not to overcrowd.

6. Repeat until all nuggets are coated. Optionally, you can spray the chicken nuggets with avocado oil before air frying for a crispy outer layer.

7. Air fry at 400F for 15-18 minutes, flipping halfway.

8. Serve the nuggets with your favorite dipping sauce!

EASY AIR FRYER LEMON CHICKEN RECIPE

Yield 2-3 servings | Total Time: 15 Min

This is my go-to chicken recipe if I need a topping for salads! Sometimes we get on a health kick and we want light meals for dinner. So that's when I reach for this recipe to serve over one of my salads!

INGREDIENTS

- 3 large boneless. skinless chicken breasts
- 3 cloves of garlic, minced
- 2 tablespoons avocado oil
- 1 lemon, zested then juiced
- 1/4 cup fresh parsley, chopped
- 1/2 teaspoon salt
- 1/4 teaspoon pepper

INSTRUCTIONS

1. Set your air fryer to 375°F (190°C) and allow it to preheat while you prepare the chicken.

2. Cut the chicken breasts into thin cutlets or use a meat mallet to pound them thin.

3. Dry the chicken slices with a paper towel, and then season evenly with salt and pepper on both sides. This step is crucial for getting tender, juicy chicken!

4. In a mixing bowl, coat the chicken cutlets with 1 tablespoon of avocado oil, ensuring they are well-covered.

5. Place the chicken cutlets in the air fryer basket in a single layer, ensuring they are not crowded. Cook for 6 minutes, flip the slices, and cook for an additional 6 minutes or until they are cooked through and golden brown.

6. While the chicken is cooking, heat the remaining 1 tablespoon of avocado oil in a small pan over medium heat. Add minced garlic and sauté for about 1 minute until fragrant. Add lemon zest and lemon juice to the pan, allowing it to deglaze. Remove from the heat.

7. Once the chicken is cooked through, transfer it to a serving dish and pour the delicious lemon garlic sauce over the top.

8. Sprinkle fresh parsley over the chicken, and serve the air-fried lemon chicken warm. Enjoy this flavorful and quick dish!

PERSIAN GREEK YOGURT-MARINATED CHICKEN KABOB

Yield: 2 Servings | Total time: 50 minutes (marinating time 30 mins.)

I grew up eating this Persian Greek yogurt marinated chicken kabob recipe once a week. My mom and dad would make it in the kitchen together, and it always came out so juicy. I now make it for my family and everyone loves it!

INGREDIENTS

- 1.25 lb chicken breast, cut into cubes
- 1 small yellow onion, roughly chopped
- ⅓ cup Greek yogurt
- 2 tablespoons lemon juice
- ½ teaspoon garlic powder
- ½ teaspoon paprika
- ½ teaspoon turmeric
- ½ teaspoon salt
- ½ teaspoon pepper
- ½ teaspoon saffron

INSTRUCTIONS

1. Add the onion, Greek yogurt, lemon juice, garlic powder, paprika, turmeric, salt, and pepper to the bowl of a food processor or blender. Blend until the mixture is well combined and the onion is chopped.

2. Place the chicken in a large bowl. Add the marinade to the chicken and toss to coat the chicken.

3. If your saffron is in threads, you can lightly crush the threads using a mortar and pestle to break them down. This helps release the flavors more efficiently. Place the 1/2 teaspoon of saffron into a small bowl or cup. Add 2-3 tablespoons of warm (not boiling) water to the saffron. The water should turn a rich golden-yellow color.

4. Add the bloomed saffron into the bowl with the chicken. If there is any leftover saffron left in the bowl, just add a bit more warm water, swirl it and add it back into the chicken.

5. Cover and let this mixture marinate for at least 30 minutes or, if time allows, overnight.

6. Heat 2 tablespoons avocado oil in a large skillet over medium-high heat. Once hot, add the chicken and cook for 3-4 minutes on each side until golden on the outside and juicy on the inside. Make sure the chicken's internal temperature is at least 165F.

7. Serve this with my fluffy white rice recipe (see page 124).

EASY & QUICK CHEESEBURGERS IN THE AIR FRYER

Yield: 4 Servings | Total Time: 20 Min

INGREDIENTS

- 1 lb lean (80/20) ground beef
- 1 tablespoon melted butter
- 1/2 teaspoon salt
- 1/2 teaspoon pepper
- 1/2 teaspoon garlic powder

Other Ingredients:

- 2 shallots, diced
- 2 teaspoon avocado oil
- 1 tomato, sliced for burger topping
- Pickles, sliced for burger toppings
- 4 buns, any kind
- 4 cheese slices

Sauce:

- 1/3 cup mayo
- 2 tablespoons ketchup
- 2 tablespoons mustard
- 2 tablespoons relish

When I was pregnant, I needed a burger at least 2x a week. I couldn't go out to get them that often so I learned different ways to make it at home. This air fryer version is probably the best way to make a burger!

INSTRUCTIONS

1. Preheat your air fryer to 380F.

2. Dice your shallot. Heat a skillet over medium heat, add 2 teaspoons of avocado oil. Once it's warm, add your diced shallot into the skillet to cook. Continue stirring continuously for about 7-9 minutes until translucent. Set the shallot aside for the sauce.

3. Divide the ground beef into 4 equal portions and shape each portion into a patty about 1/2-inch thick. Press a small indent in the center of each patty with your thumb. Make sure to press the patties firmly, as they will puff up slightly during cooking.

4. Place the burgers in a single layer in your air fryer basket.

5. Cook at 380F for 10 minutes, flipping halfway (after 5 minutes).

6. After 10 minutes, add a layer of cheese and cook for an additional 1 minute to melt the cheese.

7. While the burgers are cooking, make the sauce by mixing together the mayo, ketchup, mustard and relish until well combined.

8. To assemble the burgers, place the bun on the bottom, add sauce, burger patty, tomato, grilled shallot, lettuce, pickles and the bun on top. Enjoy warm!

PAN-SEARED STEAK

Yield: 2 Servings | Total Time: 35 Min

This is the only seared steak recipe I use. It comes out perfect every time and it's actually really quick start to finish!

INGREDIENTS

- 2 steak filets (such as NY strip)
- 1/4 teaspoon salt
- 1/8 teaspoon black pepper
- 2 tablespoons olive oil
- 2 tablespoons butter
- 6 cloves of garlic, crushed
- 6 sprigs of thyme

INSTRUCTIONS

1. Prepare the steak by letting it rest at room temperature for about 15 minutes.
2. Pat the steak dry with paper towels to remove any excess moisture.
3. Season both sides of the steak evenly with salt and pepper.
4. Heat a heavy skillet over medium-high heat. Once the pan is warm, add the olive oil.
5. Swirl the oil in the pan to coat it evenly.
6. Carefully place the seasoned, room temperature steak in the hot skillet.
7. Sear for about 2 minutes on one side (without moving it).
8. Flip the steak and cook for an additional 2 minutes for medium-rare.
9. Use tongs to turn the steak onto its side. Hold it steady with the tongs and cook each side for 1 minute to brown the edges.
10. Turn the heat to low, add your butter, whole garlic cloves, and sprigs of thyme to the skillet.
11. Tilt the skillet slightly and use a spoon to scoop up the juices from the pan and pour them over the steak for about 1-2 minutes. This helps infuse the steak with flavor.
12. Check the doneness of the steak by gently pressing on it. If it feels like a cheek, it's rare; if it feels like a chin, it's medium; and if it feels like a forehead, it's well done! Alternatively, you can use a instant-read thermometer.

    Note: Feel free to adjust the seasoning and cooking times according to your personal taste preferences and the thickness of your steak.
13. Allow the steak to rest for 5-10 minutes before slicing. Just place it on a cutting board with foil over it.
14. Look at the lines or fibers running through the steak. Cut the steak into slices that go across those lines, not in the same direction as them. This will make the meat more tender. Serve!

SIZZLING STEAK FAJITAS

Yield: 4 Servings | Total Time: 30 Min

INGREDIENTS

Steak:

- 1 pound flat iron steak
- 2 teaspoons chili powder
- 1 teaspoon cumin
- 1 teaspoon paprika
- 2 teaspoons garlic powder
- 1 teaspoon salt
- 1/2 teaspoon black pepper
- 2 tablespoons avocado oil
- 1 lime, juiced

Fajita Vegetables:

- 1 tablespoon avocado oil
- 1 red bell pepper, cut into strips
- 1 yellow bell pepper, cut into strips
- 1 green bell pepper, cut into strips
- 1 red onion, peeled and sliced into small strips
- 1 lime, juiced
- 1/2 teaspoon salt
- 1/2 teaspoon black pepper

To Serve:

- 6 tortillas, warmed

INSTRUCTIONS

1. In a small bowl, combine the chili powder, cumin, paprika, garlic powder, salt, and black pepper. Rub this seasoning mixture all over the steak.

2. Heat a large skillet over medium-high heat and add 2 tablespoons of avocado oil.

3. Place the steak in the skillet and cook until a crust forms, about 2-3 minutes. Flip and cook for another 2-3 minutes.

4. Remove the steak from the skillet and place it on a cutting board. Cover with foil and let it rest for about 10 minutes.

5. In the same skillet, add the remaining 1 tablespoon of avocado oil.

6. Add the sliced onion and bell peppers. Cook for about 5 minutes, stirring occasionally, until the vegetables are tender.

7. Season with salt, pepper, and juice of 1 lime. Remove from heat and set aside.

8. After resting, slice the steak into 1/4-inch strips. Look at the lines or fibers running through the steak. Cut the steak into slices that go across those lines, not in the same direction as them. This will make the meat more tender.

9. Drizzle juice of lime over the sliced steak for extra flavor.

10. Tuck the steak and veggies into warmed tortillas and serve.

Jazz's Tricks

- Enhance your fajitas with sour cream, guacamole, avocado, salsa, or hot sauce.
- Use leftovers in scrambled eggs for a delicious breakfast.

KOREAN BEEF LETTUCE WRAPS

Yield: 4 Servings | Total Time: 20 Min

INGREDIENTS

- 1 tablespoon avocado oil
- 3 cloves garlic, minced
- 1 lb ground beef
- 2 teaspoons ground ginger
- 1 teaspoon sesame oil
- 1/4 cup soy sauce
- 3 tablespoons brown sugar
- 1 teaspoon sweet chili sauce
- 1/4 teaspoon salt
- 1/4 teaspoon pepper
- 2 green onions, thinly sliced
- 1 teaspoon sesame seeds for garnish
- 1 head of butter lettuce
- 1/4 cup shaved carrots (optional garnish)

INSTRUCTIONS

1. Heat a large skillet over medium-high heat.
2. Once the pan is hot, add the avocado oil.
3. Swirl the oil in the pan, and once the oil feels warm, add the minced garlic and stir for about 30 seconds until fragrant.
4. Add the ground beef and continuously stir for 5 minutes, make sure to crumble the beef as it's cooking. Once it's brown, drain the excess fat.
5. Stir in the ginger, sesame oil, soy sauce, brown sugar, sweet chili sauce, salt and pepper.
6. Continue to cook over medium-high heat for about 5 more minutes to allow the flavors to meld. Stir occasionally.
7. Scoop the ground beef on top of the butter lettuce, sprinkle with green onion, sesame seeds, shaved carrots and enjoy!

PERSIAN BEEF KABOB

Yield: 4 Servings | Total Time: 30 Min

INGREDIENTS

- 1 white onion
- 1 lb ground beef
- 1 1/2 teaspoon sumac + 1 teaspoon for topping
- 1/2 teaspoon salt
- 1/4 teaspoon pepper
- 1/4 teaspoon garlic powder
- 1/4 teaspoon turmeric
- 1 teaspoon avocado oil
- 1 (14.5 oz) can of whole or crushed tomato

INSTRUCTIONS

1. Roughly chop the white onion to fit into a food processor. Process/blend for about 30 seconds until crushed. Alternatively, you can grate the onion using a cheese grater.

2. In a large bowl, combine the grated onion, ground beef, sumac (1 teaspoon), salt, pepper, garlic powder, and turmeric. Mix thoroughly with your hands until thoroughly combined.

3. Pour the avocado oil into a large non-stick skillet and spread it evenly across the entire bottom of the pan. Remember, don't turn the pan on the heat yet!

4. Place the beef mixture into the skillet on top of the avocado oil. Using your hands, flatten the meat evenly across the bottom of the skillet, about 1/4 inch thick, allowing it to come up the sides a little. This will help counteract the meat puffing up as it cooks.

5. Using a spatula, cut the flattened meat into 2-inch wide strips across the pan. Then, cut it once down the middle to create kabob strips.

6. Sprinkle 1/2 teaspoon of sumac evenly over the meat.

7. Now, place the skillet on medium-high heat. Cook for 15 minutes without covering the pan. Rotate the skillet about 30 degrees every 5 minutes to ensure even cooking.

8. After 15 minutes, flip each kabob strip. Sprinkle the remaining 1/2 teaspoon of sumac evenly over the meat.

9. Cook the flipped side for another 5 minutes.

10. Pour the can of whole or crushed tomatoes (including the juice) evenly over the kabobs.

11. Cover the skillet with a lid and turn off the heat. Cook for an additional 5 minutes until the tomatoes are heated through.

12. Serve the Persian pan kabob with on pita, with yogurt or my fluffy rice (see page 124)

GREEK-STYLE CHICKEN BURGERS

Yield: 4 Burgers | Total Time: 27 Min

INGREDIENTS

- 1/3 small red onion, chopped
- 3 garlic cloves
- 1 lb ground chicken
- 1/3 cup crumbled feta cheese
- 1 lemon, zested
- 1 teaspoon dried oregano
- 1 teaspoon sumac
- 1 teaspoon dried mint
- 1/2 teaspoon salt
- 1/2 teaspoon pepper
- 1 tablespoon avocado oil
- Creamy cucumber dill sauce for serving (see page 186)

INSTRUCTIONS

1. In a large bowl or food processor, combine the chopped onion and garlic. Pulse a few times until mostly chopped, making sure there are no large clumps.

2. Add the ground chicken, crumbled feta, lemon zest, oregano, sumac, mint, salt, and pepper to the food processor bowl where you pulsed the onion and garlic. Pulse everything together a few times until all ingredients are well combined.

3. Divide the ground chicken into 4 equal portions and shape each portion into a patty about 1/2 inch thick. Press a small indent in the center of each patty with your thumb. Make sure to press the patties firmly, as they will puff up slightly during cooking.

4. Heat 1 tablespoon avocado oil in a large skillet over medium-high heat.

5. Once the oil is hot in the pan, add the patties to the skillet. Cook for about 5-6 minutes on each side, or until the burgers are browned and have an internal temperature of 165°F (74°C). Avoid flipping the patties back and forth to allow a nice sear.

6. Remove the burgers from the skillet and let them rest for a few minutes before serving.

7. Serve with the creamy cucumber dill sauce (see page 186)

Jazz's Tricks

- Use ground turkey as a substitute for the ground chicken.
- If you prefer a more even cook, you can use a meat thermometer to check that the patties are fully cooked.
- Leftover patties can be stored in an airtight container in the refrigerator for up to 3 days. Reheat in a skillet or microwave before serving.

SAVORY PARMESAN CHICKEN MEATBALLS

Yield: About 20 Meatballs | Total Time: 35 Min

INGREDIENTS

- 1 lb ground chicken
- 1/2 onion, diced
- 1/4 cup breadcrumbs
- 2 garlic cloves, minced
- 1 egg
- 1/4 cup finely grated parmesan cheese
- 3 tablespoons ketchup
- 1 teaspoon salt
- 1/4 teaspoon pepper
- 1 tablespoon minced parsley

INSTRUCTIONS

1. Preheat your oven to 400°F (200°C).

2. In a large bowl, combine the ground chicken, diced onion, minced garlic, bread crumbs, egg, grated parmesan cheese, ketchup, salt, pepper, and minced parsley.

3. Use your hands to mix everything together until well combined. Be careful not to over-mix, as this can make the meatballs tough.

4. Scoop about 1 tablespoon of the meat mixture and roll it into a ball. Place each meatball onto a parchment paper-lined baking sheet. Continue until all the mixture is used.

5. Bake the meatballs in the preheated oven for 20 minutes, or until they are browned and cooked through.

6. Let the meatballs cool slightly before serving. Enjoy them as a main dish, in a pasta sauce, or with a side of vegetables.

Jazz's Tricks

- You can use ground beef, turkey, or pork instead of ground chicken if preferred.
- Store leftover meatballs in an airtight container in the refrigerator for up to 4 days. Reheat in the oven or microwave before serving.
- Meatballs freeze well. Place cooled meatballs in a freezer bag or container and freeze for up to 3 months. Reheat from frozen in a 350°F (175°C) oven for 20-25 minutes.

SPICED MEDITERRANEAN CHICKEN SHAWARMA

Yield: 4 Servings | Total Time: 55 Min (includes marinating time)

INGREDIENTS

Chicken:

- 1 lb boneless skinless chicken thighs
- 1/4 cup olive oil
- 1 lemon, zested then juiced
- 1 teaspoon garlic powder
- 1 teaspoon ground cumin
- 1 teaspoon paprika
- 1 teaspoon salt
- 1/2 teaspoon ground cinnamon
- Avocado oil spray
- 2 tablespoons fresh parsley, chopped (optional)

INSTRUCTIONS

1. Place the chicken in a large airtight container or a Ziploc bag.

2. Add the olive oil, lemon juice, lemon zest, garlic powder, ground cumin, paprika, salt, and ground cinnamon to the chicken and mix everything well to ensure the chicken is evenly coated with the marinade.

3. Seal the container and refrigerate for at least 30 minutes, up to 12 hours. The longer you marinate, the more flavorful the chicken will be.

4. Preheat your air fryer to 400°F (200°C).

5. Remove the marinated chicken from the fridge and let it sit at room temperature for 5 minutes.

6. Spray the air fryer basket with avocado oil spray.

7. Place the chicken in the air fryer basket in a single layer.

8. Air fry for 15 minutes, or until the chicken is crispy on the outside and cooked through. The internal temperature should reach 165°F (74°C).

9. Once cooked, transfer the chicken to a cutting board and cover with foil. Let it rest for 5 minutes before slicing.

10. Sprinkle the chopped fresh parsley over the chicken.

Jazz's Tips

- Set a reminder on your phone to marinate the chicken the night before. This way, you'll have flavorful chicken ready to cook the next day.
- Store any leftover chicken in an airtight container in the refrigerator for up to 3 days.
- To reheat, microwave the chicken for 60 seconds or use the air fryer's "reheat" setting for 3 minutes.

GREEK TURKEY BURGERS

Yield: 4 burgers | Total Time: 23 Min

Being Middle Eastern, I love to incorporate those flavors into my recipes. Whenever I make these, I serve them with a creamy yogurt sauce and it's so fun on burgers, salads or for meal prep!

INGREDIENTS

- 1 lb ground turkey
- 3 garlic cloves, minced
- 1/3 cup crumbled feta cheese
- 1/3 small red onion, finely chopped
- Zest of 1 lemon, about 1 teaspoon
- 1 teaspoon oregano
- 1 teaspoon sumac
- 2 tablespoons fresh mint
- 1/2 teaspoon salt
- 1/2 teaspoon black pepper
- 1 tablespoon avocado oil (for cooking)

INSTRUCTIONS

1. Mince the garlic and chop the red onion finely.

2. In a large bowl, combine the ground turkey, garlic, crumbled feta cheese, finely chopped red onion, lemon zest, oregano, sumac, dried mint, salt and black pepper. Mix well until all ingredients are evenly incorporated.

3. Divide the mixture into 4-8 equal portions, depending on your desired burger size. Roll each portion into a ball, then gently flatten to about 3/4 inch thickness. Press a small indentation in the center of each patty to ensure even cooking.

4. Heat a large skillet over medium-high heat and add 1 tablespoon of avocado oil. Once hot, add the burgers to the skillet. Cook for about 5-6 minutes per side without flipping too frequently to allow the burgers to brown nicely.

5. When the burgers reach an internal temperature of 165°F, remove from heat. Serve immediately with your favorite burger toppings, or tuck them into a pita with tzatziki, lettuce, and tomato.

PESTO CHICKEN SANDWICH

Yield: 2 Sandwiches | Total Time: 15 Min

This is inspired by my favorite deli in my hometown of Santa Barbara, CA. Every time I go back to visit, it's the first stop for me! It always makes me so happy!

INGREDIENTS

- 2 cups rotisserie chicken, shredded
- ½ lemon, juiced
- 1 tablespoon olive oil
- 1/2 teaspoon garlic powder
- 1/2 teaspoon onion powder
- 1/4 teaspoon chili powder
- 1/4 teaspoon black pepper
- 1/4 teaspoon salt
- 2 fresh mozzarella cheese balls, sliced
- 4 tablespoons basil pesto
- 1 large tomato, thinly sliced
- 4 tablespoons mayonnaise
- 4 slices sourdough bread

INSTRUCTIONS

1. Combine the shredded rotisserie chicken with the juice of ½ a lemon in a small bowl. Set aside.

2. Spread 1 tablespoon of mayonnaise on one side of each slice of sourdough.

3. Spread 1 tablespoon of pesto on two of the slices (on the side without mayo).

4. Add a layer of the rotisserie chicken, then the mozzarella, and tomato on top of the pesto slices.

5. Place the other slice of bread on top (mayo side facing out).

6. Heat a skillet over medium heat.

7. Place the sandwiches in the pan, with the mayo side facing down.

8. Cook for 3-4 minutes on each side, or until the bread is golden and the cheese is melted.

9. Slice the sandwiches in half and serve warm. Enjoy your delicious pesto chicken sandwich!

CRISPY AIR FRIED CHICKEN

Yield: 8 Chicken Tenders | Total Time: 25 Min

This is my go-to way to make crispy chicken. It's my favorite way to add protein on salads and you'll see this recipe reference in this book quite a lot! Use it on any salad, pasta or as a dipper into your favorite sauce like ranch or ketchup!

INGREDIENTS

- 1.25 lb chicken tenders
- 2 eggs
- 1 cup breadcrumbs (use gluten free if necessary)
- 1/2 teaspoon garlic powder
- 1/2 teaspoon paprika
- 1/2 teaspoon salt
- 1/2 teaspoon pepper

INSTRUCTIONS

1. Season your chicken tenders with salt and pepper on both sides.

2. Grab two shallow bowls. Add your eggs to one bowl, whisk to combine the eggs.

3. In the other bowl, add your breadcrumbs, garlic powder and paprika.

4. Grab the chicken tender, dip it in the egg, then into the breadcrumb mixture. Shake off any excess breading then place it aside on a cutting board.

5. Continue to complete all chicken pieces.

6. Spray your hot air fryer with a little bit of cooking oil, then lay your chicken tenders in a single layer (careful not to overlap in the air fryer).

7. Air fry at 400 degrees F for 12-15 minutes, flipping halfway through. Each air fryer is different, so I just recommend checking them at 12 minutes!

8. The chicken will be golden on the outside, and the inside will be cooked to 165F.

Fish & Seafood

Deliciously Simple Seafood Staples

Fish is the most-eaten protein in our house—we absolutely love it. The first recipe I shared on social media that went viral was for air-fried salmon, and it remains my favorite protein to cook. This section features a range of delicious fish recipes that highlight just how versatile and satisfying seafood can be. Whether you're a long-time fan or new to cooking fish, you'll find plenty of inspiration here for making meals you'll truly enjoy.

COOKBOOK / COOKBOOK / COOKBOOK / COOKBOOK /

CILANTRO LIME SHRIMP TACOS

Yield: 9-12 Tacos | Total Time: 15 Min

Cilantro lime shrimp tacos are what I ate the night I went into labor. I remember having contractions as I was eating them! Love the creamy sauce that goes on top!

INGREDIENTS

Slaw

- 4 cups of coleslaw
- 2 tablespoons mayo
- 1 teaspoon apple cider vinegar
- 1 teaspoon agave or honey
- Pinch of salt, to taste
- Pinch of pepper, to taste

Shrimp

- 16 oz shrimp, I prefer using jumbo shrimp (about 20-30 count)
- 2-3 tablespoons of taco seasoning
- 2 tablespoons avocado oil for cooking

Cilantro Lime Sauce

- 1/4 cup mayo
- 1 lime, zested + juiced
- 1/4 cup chopped cilantro
- Dash of hot sauce, more or less depending on taste preference
- Pinch of salt, to taste
- Pinch of pepper, to taste

Other Ingredients

- 9-12 tortillas of choice

INSTRUCTIONS

Slaw

1. To make the slaw, combine the coleslaw, mayo, apple cider vinegar, agave, salt and pepper together in a bowl. Mix well for 30 seconds - 60 seconds until the slaw is completely coated.

2. Make any adjustments to the flavor if needed.

Cilantro Lime Sauce

1. Into a blender or food processor, add mayo, lime juice, lime zest, cilantro, hot sauce, salt and pepper. Blend until smooth. Taste to make any adjustments and pour into a small bowl.

Shrimp

1. Ensure shrimp is thawed and deveined. Pat the shrimp dry.

2. Transfer into a bowl along with the taco seasoning. Mix well to coat all of the shrimp in the seasoning.

3. Add avocado oil to a large skillet. Heat on medium-high heat.

4. Once the oil is hot, add your shrimp, ensuring not to overcrowd the pan. Cook for 1 minute, then flip and cook for another minute.

5. Remove from the skillet and place on a plate or bowl to assemble.

Tortilla

1. To char the tortillas, just turn a gas stove on medium-high heat. Place the tortilla directly on the flame for 10-20 seconds, flip and char the other side. Set aside until all tortillas are charred.

2. Alternatively, if you do not have a gas stove, you can place the tortillas on a sheet pan and bake for 5 minutes at 300F to warm up.

3. For an easy alternative, wrap the tortillas in a moist paper towel or kitchen towel. Place in the microwave for 20-30 seconds. Enjoy warm.

AIR FRYER CRISPY PARMESAN SALMON BITES

Yield: 2 Servings | Total Time: 10 Min

INGREDIENTS

- 1 lb salmon
- 3 tablespoons olive oil
- 1/2 cup grated parmesan
- 1 teaspoon garlic powder
- 1 teaspoon paprika
- 1/4 teaspoon salt
- 1/4 teaspoon pepper
- Avocado oil spray
- Garlic mayo sauce (see page 191)

These Air Fryer Crispy Parmesan Salmon Bites went very viral on my social media pages with over millions of views for good reason. The crispy parmesan coating is so delicious! I love serving them on mashed potatoes, rice, or noodles—don't forget the garlic mayo!

INSTRUCTIONS

1. Wash your salmon filet, then place it on a paper towel. Dab it dry to remove any moisture.
2. Using a sharp knife, carefully remove the skin of the salmon if needed. Cut the salmon into 1-inch cubes. Make sure the salmon is cut into equal pieces so it all cooks evenly.
3. Add the salmon cubes to a bowl. Add 3 tablespoons of olive oil, the grated parmesan cheese, garlic powder, paprika, salt and pepper.
4. Toss it all together to coat the salmon.
5. Place the salmon in an even layer in the air fryer basket. Spray the top of the salmon with avocado oil spray to evenly coat and ensure a crispy exterior.
6. Air fry at 380F for about 6 minutes until golden brown and crispy.
7. Remove from the air fryer and drizzle with the garlic mayo sauce.

AIR FRYER SALMON WITH CRISPY ASPARAGUS

Yield: 2 Servings | Total Time: 10 Min

INGREDIENTS

Salmon Ingredients

- 1 lb salmon, cut into 2 filets
- 2 teaspoons Dijon mustard
- 1/4 teaspoon garlic powder
- 1/4 teaspoon paprika
- 1/8 teaspoon pepper
- 1 lemon

Asparagus Ingredients

- 8-10 oz of fresh asparagus
- 1 teaspoon avocado oil
- 1/4 teaspoon salt
- 1/4 teaspoon garlic powder
- 1/8 teaspoon pepper
- Zest of 1 lemon, use the zest from the lemon before you juice it

Air Fryer Salmon with Crispy Asparagus was my very first cooking class demo! It's crazy how easy it is. A lot of first-time cooks said it actually made them confident about actually cooking fish. This is our family go-to when we are low on time for a weeknight keto-friendly, low-carb dinner.

INSTRUCTIONS

Salmon Directions

1. Cut the salmon into two filets (if they aren't already).
2. Pat the salmon filets dry with a paper towel.
3. Spread the Dijon mustard generously on each filet with a spoon, also rub the sides!
4. In a small bowl, combine the garlic powder, paprika, and black pepper for the salmon. Sprinkle the seasoning on top of each piece of salmon.
5. Place in a sprayed air fryer, skin side down.
6. Air fry at 395F for 12 minutes.
7. Remove from the heat and let it sit for about 5 minutes.
8. Serve each filet with 1/2 of the lemon juiced on top

Asparagus Directions

1. While the salmon is cooking, wash the asparagus, and cut the bottom 1-2 inches off of the asparagus.
2. Toss the asparagus in avocado oil, salt, garlic powder and lemon zest.
3. Place the asparagus into the air fryer.
4. Air fry (in the same container as the salmon) at 395F for 5 minutes.
5. Remove immediately as they will continue cooking.
6. Serve alongside the salmon.

PESTO-CRUSTED SALMON RECIPE

Yield: 2 Servings | Total Time: 23 Min

This Pesto-Crusted Salmon was a dish I made at least once a week when I used to be a private chef for professional athletes. They asked for it every game day as their pre-game meal along with a big bowl of pasta!

INGREDIENTS

Salmon

- 1lb fresh salmon
- 2-3 tablespoons homemade pesto
- 3 tablespoons breadcrumbs
- 1 tablespoon lemon juice, about 1/2 lemon
- 1/8 teaspoon salt
- 1/8 teaspoon black pepper

Homemade Pesto Sauce

- 2 cups fresh basil
- 1/3 cup grated parmesan cheese
- 1/2 cup walnuts
- 3 tablespoons extra virgin olive oil
- 2 tablespoons lemon juice
- 2 tablespoons water
- 1 teaspoon garlic, minced
- 1/2 teaspoon salt
- 1/4 teaspoon pepper

INSTRUCTIONS

Homemade Pesto Sauce

1. Toast the nuts on medium heat on a skillet for about 3-4 minutes until fragrant.
2. Into a food processor or high-powered blender, add all of the ingredients: fresh basil, parmesan cheese, walnuts, extra virgin olive oil, lemon juice, garlic, salt, and pepper (exclude water).
3. Blend for 20-30 seconds.
4. Add 2 tablespoons of water (or more) until desired consistency is met.
5. Remember to taste your pesto to ensure it doesn't need any other seasoning!
6. Store in an airtight container in the fridge for up to 7 days, or freeze for up to 2 months.

Salmon

1. Preheat the oven to 425 degrees Fahrenheit.
2. Place salmon skin-side down on a parchment paper-lined baking sheet. Spread about a 1/4-inch layer of the pesto on top of the salmon.
3. Add lemon juice and the remaining seasoning.
4. Sprinkle the breadcrumbs on top as the last layer.
5. Bake the salmon for about 12-15 minutes (12 for a smaller filet or 15 for a larger).
6. Broil the salmon on low for an additional 3 minutes after the timer has gone off, allowing the breadcrumbs to crisp.

Jazz's Tricks

- I like using Panko breadcrumbs for this. But feel free to use any kind you want. Substitute for gluten-free breadcrumbs if necessary.
- If you don't like salmon, substitute this for any other fish (i.e., bass, snapper, grouper)
- To air fry, just air fry at 400F for about 10-12 mins.
- Substitute the parmesan for nutritional yeast if you are dairy-free.
- Substitute the parmesan cheese for asiago or pecorino romano cheese.
- I prefer using fresh garlic but if you only have pre-minced garlic or garlic powder, that is fine.

COPYCAT GORDON RAMSAY'S PAN-SEARED SALMON

Yield: 2 Servings | Total Time: 18 Min

I admire Gordon Ramsay as a chef, and I have to say, his recipe for pan-seared salmon is the best one I have ever tried. It feels like you are eating at a restaurant! Everyone needs this recipe!

INGREDIENTS

- 2 salmon filets
- 1/4 teaspoon salt
- 1/8 teaspoon black pepper
- 1 tablespoon olive oil
- 1 tablespoon butter
- 4 cloves of garlic
- 4 sprigs of thyme
- 1 lemon, zested and juiced

INSTRUCTIONS

1. Let the salmon come to room temperature for 10 minutes before cooking.
2. Pat the salmon dry. If your salmon has skin on it, make sure to pat that side especially dry.
3. If your salmon has skin, place the salmon on a cutting board, skin side up, and use a knife to make shallow cuts in the fish skin, about 1/4 inch deep. This will prevent the salmon from curling. If your salmon does not have skin, you can still score the salmon.
4. Season both sides with salt, paprika, and pepper, rubbing the seasoning into the scoring.
5. Heat a skillet over medium heat.
6. Wait until the skillet is hot, then add olive oil.
7. Once the oil is heated, add the salmon to the oil, skin-side down. Press down gently with a spatula. Cook for 2 minutes on one side, then flip and cook for another 2 minutes on the other side.
8. Flip the salmon so the skin-side is down (again).
9. Add 1 tablespoon of butter, 4 cloves of garlic and 4 sprigs of thyme.
10. Reduce the heat to low and use a spoon to scoop up the juices from the pan and pour them over the salmon with the herbed butter for about 6 minutes.
11. Finish with lemon zest, lemon juice, parsley and the final herbed butter drizzled on top.

GRILLED MAHI MAHI WITH MANGO SALSA

Yield: 2-4 Servings | Total Time: 25 Min

We used to have a neighbor with a mango tree, and the mangos constantly fell in our backyard. This mango salsa was always a go-to for us whenever we got some mango! It goes well with any fish, and it gets better as it sits in the fridge!

INGREDIENTS

Seared Fish

- 2 mahi mahi filets
- 2 tablespoons mayonnaise
- 1/2 teaspoon salt
- 1/4 teaspoon black pepper
- 2 tablespoons olive oil or avocado oil
- Juice of 1 lime

Mango Salsa

- 1 ripe mango, diced
- 1 red bell pepper, diced
- 1/2 red onion, diced
- 1 jalapeño, seeds removed and diced
- Juice of 1 lime
- 1/4 cup chopped cilantro
- 1/2 teaspoon salt
- 1/4 teaspoon black pepper
- 2 tablespoons olive oil

INSTRUCTIONS

1. Start by preparing the mango salsa. In a medium bowl, combine the diced mango, red bell pepper, red onion, and jalapeño.

3. Add the lime juice, chopped cilantro, salt, and pepper.

4. Drizzle the olive oil over the salsa and mix until well combined.

5. Set the mango salsa aside to let the flavors meld while you cook the mahi mahi.

6. To prepare the mahi mahi, remove the blood line. To do this, just identify the blood line: it's a dark, reddish-brown strip of tissue running along the center of the fish. Use a sharp knife to remove it.

7. Pat the fish dry with paper towels. This is really important to make sure the fish doesn't stick to your grill pan.

8. Season both sides of the filets evenly with salt and black pepper.

9. Take 1 tablespoon of mayonnaise and spread on one side of the filets. Spread it evenly with a pastry brush or a spoon.

10. Heat a grill pan over medium-high heat. Wait a few minutes, then add the avocado oil.

11. Once the oil is hot, carefully place the seasoned mahi mahi filets in the pan. Place them away from you so the oil doesn't splatter all over yourself.

12. Sear the fish for about 3 minutes on one side until it develops a nice crust.

13. While the fish is searing, dry the other side with a paper towel, sprinkle it with salt and pepper and spread mayonnaise on it.

14. Flip the filets and cook for another 3 minutes on the other side until the fish is cooked through.

15. In the last minutes of cooking, squeeze the juice of one lime over the fish.

16. Once the fish is cooked through and nicely seared on both sides, remove it from the grill pan and place it on serving plates.

17. Spoon the fresh mango salsa generously over each piece of mahi mahi.

18. Serve the grilled mahi mahi with mango salsa immediately and enjoy!

EASY TROPICAL CEVICHE DE MANGO

Yield: 4-8 People | Total Time: 45 Min

INGREDIENTS

- 1 lb fresh snapper (or any other fish)
- 1 mango, diced
- 1 red onion, diced
- 5 scallions, chopped
- 1 bunch of parsley, chopped
- 6 fresh limes, zested + juiced
- 2 tablespoons apple cider vinegar
- 2 teaspoons salt
- 2 teaspoons pepper
- 1 teaspoon garlic powder

INSTRUCTIONS

1. Dice the fish into uniform, bite-sized pieces.
2. Add all of the ingredients to a big bowl, preferably with a lid. Mix the ceviche well.
3. Store in the fridge for at least 30 minutes to allow the flavors to develop and the fish to cook.
4. Remove from the fridge & enjoy with your favorite chips!

This easy tropical mango ceviche was something we made all of the time when my husband was a fishing charter captain! He always brought home fresh fish whenever he got back from fishing! It's so great with chips!

CRISPY AIR FRYER BANG BANG SALMON BITES

Yield: 2 | Total time: 15 Min

These Bang Bang Salmon Bites in the air fryer is one of my husband's favorite ways to eat salmon. He loves to make it extra spicy with more sriracha drizzle on top!

INGREDIENTS

For the Salmon

- 1 lb salmon, cut into cubes
- 1/4 teaspoon paprika
- 1/4 teaspoon garlic powder
- 1/4 teaspoon ground ginger
- 1/4 teaspoon salt
- 1/8 teaspoon pepper

For the Bang Bang Sauce

- 1/3 cup mayonnaise
- 2 tablespoons sriracha
- 1/4 cup sweet chili sauce
- Squeeze of lemon

For Garnish

- Chopped chives

INSTRUCTIONS

1. Dry the salmon with a paper towel then cut the salmon into bite-sized, 1-inch cubes.

2. In a medium bowl, toss the salmon cubes with 1/4 teaspoon paprika, 1/4 teaspoon garlic powder, 1/4 teaspoon ground ginger, 1/4 teaspoon salt, and 1/8 teaspoon pepper until evenly coated.

3. Prepare the bang bang sauce. In a small bowl, mix together 1/3 cup mayonnaise, 2 tablespoons sriracha, 1/4 cup sweet chili sauce, and a squeeze of lemon. Set that aside.

4. Add 2-3 tablespoons of the prepared Crispy Air Fryer Bang Bang Salmon Bites. Toss gently to coat the salmon evenly with the sauce.

5. Preheat the air fryer to 400 degrees Fahrenheit.

6. Spray the air fryer basket with avocado oil cooking spray.

7. Place the salmon cubes in a single layer in the air fryer basket, careful not to overcrowd the pan. Work in batches.

8. Air fry at 400 degrees Fahrenheit for 8 minutes, shaking the basket halfway through the cooking time for even cooking.

9. Transfer the cooked salmon bites to a serving platter.

10. Drizzle the remaining bang bang sauce over the salmon bites.

11. Garnish with chopped chives.

LEMON GARLIC BUTTER AIR FRIED SALMON

Yield: 2 Servings | Total time: 15 Min

Perfect for weeknights on top of some buttered noodles or a big salad! I craved this recipe at the end of my pregnancy, it's so juicy!

INGREDIENTS

- 2 salmon filets
- 2 tbsp butter, melted
- 2 cloves of garlic, or 1 tsp garlic powder
- 2 tsp lemon zest
- 1 lemon, juiced
- 1/4 tsp salt
- parsley (optional to finish)
- pesto (optional, see page 188)

INSTRUCTIONS

1. Dab your salmon dry with a paper towel.
2. In a small bowl, mix together the salmon, slightly melted butter, garlic, lemon zest, lemon juice and salt. Mix to combine.
3. Pour the lemon garlic butter sauce on top of the salmon filets.
4. Place the salmon in the air fryer. Air fry at 390F for 10 minutes until salmon internal temperature is 145F.
5. Add a spoonful of pesto on top for an added pop of flavor once it's cooked.

GARLIC BROWN SUGAR GLAZED SALMON

Yield: 2 Servings | Total Time: 30 Min

I swear this is how restaurants make the salmon on the menu. The glaze is sticky, sweet, salty and pops with a ton of flavor. My daughter loves this one too, i'll serve it with rice and some avocado on the side!

INGREDIENTS

- 1 lb salmon filets (2 filets)
- 1/4 cup soy sauce
- 2 tablespoons brown sugar
- 2 tablespoons avocado oil (1 tablespoon for cooking and 1 tablespoon for marinade)
- 1/2 teaspoon garlic powder
- 1/2 teaspoon ginger powder
- 1/4 teaspoon salt
- 1/4 teaspoon pepper

INSTRUCTIONS

1. In a small mixing bowl, combine the soy sauce, brown sugar, 1 tablespoon avocado oil, garlic powder, ginger powder, salt, and pepper. Stir until the brown sugar is completely dissolved and all ingredients are welled mixed.

2. Pat salmon filets dry with a paper towel.

3. Place the salmon filets in a shallow dish or a resealable plastic bag.

4. Pour the marinade over the salmon, ensuring the filets are fully coated.

5. Let the salmon marinate in the refrigerator for at least 15 minutes. For best results, marinate for up to 1 hour.

6. Heat a stainless steel pan over medium heat. Once the pan is hot, add 1 tablespoon of avocado to the pan. Add a piece of parchment paper that will fit both pieces of salmon. Flip the parchment paper to coat both sides with oil.

7. Once the parchment paper is hot, place the salmon filets on it, skin-side down. Cook the salmon for 4 minutes until the skin is crispy. Carefully flip the salmon filets and cook on the other side for an additional 4 minutes. Reduce the heat to medium and continue to cook until the salmon reaches an internal temperature of 145°F (63°C) or flakes easily with a fork.

8. Remove the salmon from the pan, let it rest for a few minutes, finish with scallions and enjoy with your favorite sides!

AIR FRYER SUMAC SALMON

Yield: 2 Servings | Total time: 14 Min

INGREDIENTS

- 2 salmon filets
- ⅛ teaspoon saffron + 1 tablespoon warm water
- 2 teaspoons olive oil
- 2 teaspoons butter
- ½ teaspoon salt
- ¼ teaspoon pepper
- Juice of ½ lemon
- 2 teaspoons sumac

Sumac and saffron are two flavors we add into so many dishes in Persian cuisine. My mom taught me this recipe, and it's so unique! I remember she made it for me right after I gave birth because of the endless benefits of saffron and sumac!

INSTRUCTIONS

1. Pat your salmon filets dry.

2. Score the salmon with a sharp knife to allow the seasonings to flavor the salmon more deeply.

3. If your saffron is in threads, you can lightly crush the threads using a mortar and pestle to break them down. Place the 1/8 teaspoon of saffron into a small bowl or cup. Add 1 tablespoon of warm water to the saffron. The water should turn a rich golden-yellow color. Brush it evenly on your salmon.

4. Drizzle the salmon with olive oil. Sprinkle the salmon with salt, pepper, and lemon juice, then sumac. Add the butter right on top (not melted) in 1 teaspoon scoops. Allow it to seep into the salmon while cooking.

5. Air fry at 390F for 9 minutes or until the salmon has reached an internal temp of 145 (for consistency)

SMOKED SALMON DIP

Yield: 2 Cups | Total Time: 10 Min

INGREDIENTS

- 8 oz cream cheese, softened
- 1/4 cup finely chopped capers
- 1/4 cup finely chopped red onion
- 6 oz smoked salmon, chopped
- 2 tablespoons chopped chives
- 1 tablespoon lemon juice
- Salt and pepper to taste

I learned how to make this recipe when I traveled to Alaska to learn about Copper River Salmon. We visited locals that had a smoker and got to taste that fresh smoked salmon. Soon after, a group of us went to a kitchen to test out this recipe and it's my favorite way to enjoy smoked fish!

INSTRUCTIONS

1. In a large mixing bowl, combine the softened cream cheese, finely chopped capers, finely chopped red onion, chopped smoked salmon, chopped chives, and lemon juice.

2. Mash the ingredients together with a fork until well combined and creamy.

3. Season with salt and pepper to taste.

4. Serve immediately with your favorite crackers, veggies, or spread on a bagel. Enjoy!

Dressings & Sauces

Easy, Healthy, and Bursting with Flavor

A great sauce or dressing can transform any meal, bringing flavors together and adding a delicious finishing touch. Unfortunately, store-bought options often come loaded with less-than-ideal ingredients, and the healthier alternatives can be expensive. That's why I'm excited to share these homemade recipes. They're all about keeping things healthy, affordable, and easy to whip up at home. Use them to enhance your salads, bowls, and proteins, or as tasty dips. These sauces and dressings are sure to become staples in your kitchen.

COOKBOOK / COOKBOOK / COOKBOOK / COOKBOOK /

QUICK AND EASY HOMEMADE BALSAMIC VINAIGRETTE

Yield: 1 cup | Total Time: 3 Min

INGREDIENTS

- ¼ cup balsamic vinegar
- ¾ cup extra virgin olive oil
- 1 tablespoon Dijon mustard
- 1 garlic clove, minced or 1 teaspoon garlic powder
- 1 teaspoon honey or maple syrup
- ¼ teaspoon salt
- ⅛ teaspoon pepper

This balsamic vinaigrette is my go-to salad dressing. I don't remember the last time I bought a store-bought dressing. It's a great way to use up your leftover mustard! Made with just 7 ingredients in less than 5 minutes, it's never been easier to whip up your own dressing!

INSTRUCTIONS

1. In a small mason jar or a container with a lid, add the balsamic balsamic vinegar, Dijon mustard, minced garlic, and optional honey or maple syrup. Whisk or shake to combine the ingredients together. Then gradually add in the oil while whisking.

2. Taste the dressing to see if you need to make any adjustments. Add more salt, pepper, vinegar, or sweetener to balance the flavors to your preference.

3. Store it in the fridge for up to 5 days. Enjoy the dressing on your favorite salad, roasted vegetables, or grilled meats!

APPLE CIDER VINAIGRETTE

Yield: about 3/4 cup | Total Time: 10 Min

INGREDIENTS

- 1/2 cup olive oil
- 1/4 cup apple cider vinaigrette
- 1 lime, juiced
- 2 tablespoons honey
- 1/4 teaspoon salt
- 1/4 teaspoon black pepper
- ¼ teaspoon garlic powder

INSTRUCTIONS

1. Begin by making the chicken! You can use my air-fried chicken cutlet recipe.

2. Grab a big bowl, and add the spring mix on the bottom.

3. Add the strawberries, apples, blueberries, walnuts, blue cheese and granola on top.

4. Into a jar with a lid, add the ingredients for the apple cider vinaigrette. Shake it well to combine. Taste and make any adjustments if needed.

5. Finish the salad with sliced chicken and a drizzle of apple cider vinaigrette.

6. Toss to combine & enjoy right away.

HIGH-PROTEIN RANCH DRESSING

Yield: about 1 cup | Total Time: 10 Min

INGREDIENTS

- 1 cup plain Greek yogurt (any kind)
- 1 tablespoon lemon juice
- 1 teaspoon fresh chives, minced
- 1 teaspoon fresh parsley, minced
- 1 teaspoon dried dill
- 1/2 teaspoon garlic powder
- 1/2 teaspoon onion powder
- 1/2 teaspoon salt
- 1/4 teaspoon black pepper
- 1–2 tablespoons water (optional, for thinning)

INSTRUCTIONS

1. Add all ingredients to a jar with a lid.
2. Shake vigorously until everything is well combined. Taste and adjust seasoning if needed.
3. If the dressing is too thick, add 1–2 tablespoons of water to reach your desired consistency.

Jazz's Tricks

- Substitute the Greek yogurt for a plain non-dairy yogurt

GREEN GODDESS DRESSING

Yield: about 2 cups | Total Time: 5 Min

INGREDIENTS

- 1 cup fresh basil
- 1 avocado
- 1/2 bunch of cilantro
- 1/2 bunch of parsley
- 1/4 cup fresh mint leaves
- 1/3 cup hemp seeds
- 1/4 cup nutritional yeast
- Juice of 1 lemon
- 1/4 cup olive oil
- 3 cloves garlic
- 1 shallot
- 1/2 teaspoon salt
- 1/4 teaspoon pepper
- 1/2 cup - 2/3 cup filtered water

Not only does this sauce make for the creamiest salad dressing, but it also makes for an incredible dipping sauce for sweet potato fries, salmon or chicken!

INSTRUCTIONS

1. To a blender, add all of the ingredients except the water.
2. Add about 1/2 cup filtered water and blend. Add more water 1 tablespoon at a time until desired consistency is achieved.
3. I like to blend my dressing for about 30 seconds until creamy and smooth.
4. Store in a mason jar with a lid.

MAPLE VINAIGRETTE

Yield: about 1/2 cup | Total Time: 2 Min

INGREDIENTS

- 1/4 cup extra-virgin olive oil
- 2 tablespoons apple cider vinegar
- 1 tablespoon pure maple syrup
- 1 teaspoon Dijon mustard
- Salt and black pepper to taste

INSTRUCTIONS

1. In a mason jar with a lid or a small bowl, add the olive oil, apple cider vinegar, maple syrup, Dijon mustard, salt, and pepper. Shake until combined.

CHILI LIME CREMA

Yield: about ½ cup | Total Time: 5 Min

INGREDIENTS

- 1/2 cup plain yogurt
- 3 tablespoons lime juice, about 1 lime
- 1 1/2 teaspoons Tajín seasoning
- 1/2 teaspoon chili powder

INSTRUCTIONS

1. In a small bowl, combine the yogurt, lime juice, Tajín seasoning, and chili powder.

2. Whisk until the mixture is smooth and well combined.

Jazz's Tricks

- For a thicker consistency, use plain Greek yogurt.
- Tajín seasoning can be substituted with chili lime seasoning.
- Adjust the amount of chili powder to suit your spice preference.
- Enjoy as a topping for tacos, salads, or grilled vegetables!

CARAMELIZED SHALLOT MAGIC SAUCE

Yield: about 1 cup | Total Time: 10 Min

INGREDIENTS

- 2 shallots, diced
- 6 cloves garlic, minced
- 3 tablespoons olive oil
- 2 tablespoons Dijon mustard
- 2 teaspoons honey, maple syrup, or agave
- 1/4 cup lemon juice
- 1/2 teaspoon salt
- 1/2 teaspoon pepper

INSTRUCTIONS

1. Preheat a small skillet over medium heat. Once the pan is hot, add 3 tablespoons of olive oil.

2. Add the shallots and cook for 3 minutes, stirring occasionally.

3. Add the minced garlic to the skillet. Stir for 30 seconds until the garlic becomes fragrant.

4. Lower the heat to low. Stir in the Dijon mustard, honey, lemon juice, salt, and pepper. Mix until the dressing comes together and thickens slightly.

5. Taste the dressing and adjust seasoning if needed.

6. The dressing can be served warm or cold, depending on your preference.

Jazz's Tricks

- Swap the honey for for maple syrup or agave.
- Store leftover dressing in an airtight container in the refrigerator for up to 1 week.
- To reheat, warm gently on the stove over low heat or in the microwave before serving. If the dressing thickens after refrigeration, whisk in a small amount of water, olive oil or extra lemon juice to reach your desired consistency.

CREAMY CUCUMBER DILL DIP

Yield: about 2 cups | Total Time: 5 Min

INGREDIENTS

- 2 cups plain yogurt
- 6 Persian cucumbers, peeled and diced
- 2 tablespoons dried dill, or 5 tablespoons of fresh
- 1 lemon, zested and juiced
- 2 cloves garlic, minced
- 1/2 teaspoon salt
- 1/4 teaspoon pepper

INSTRUCTIONS

1. In a medium bowl, combine the yogurt, chopped cucumber, minced garlic, dill, lemon zest, lemon juice, salt and pepper.

2. Stir everything together until well mixed.

3. Refrigerate the dip for at least 30 minutes to allow the flavors to meld. This also helps the dip to thicken slightly.

Jazz's Tricks

- If you prefer a smoother texture, you can grate the cucumber and squeeze out excess moisture before adding it to the yogurt.
- Fresh dill adds a more vibrant flavor, but dried dill works well too.
- Greek yogurt provides a thicker consistency, while dairy-free yogurt can be used for a vegan option.
- Store leftover dip in an airtight container in the refrigerator for up to 3 days. It may thicken as it sits; stir before serving.

FRESH BASIL & WALNUT PESTO

Yield: about 1 cup | Total Time: 10 Min

INGREDIENTS

- 1/2 cup walnuts
- 2 cups fresh basil leaves
- 1/3 cup grated parmesan cheese
- 2 garlic cloves
- 1/2 teaspoon salt
- 1/4 teaspoon pepper
- ¼ cup extra virgin olive oil
- 2 tablespoons lemon juice
- 2 tablespoons water

INSTRUCTIONS

1. Toast the walnuts in a dry skillet over medium heat for a few minutes until fragrant, then let them cool.

2. In a food processor, combine the fresh basil, grated parmesan cheese, toasted walnuts, garlic, salt, and pepper.

3. Add the olive oil, lemon juice, and water to the food processor.

4. Pulse the ingredients until the mixture becomes smooth and well combined, stopping to scrape down the sides of the bowl as needed.

5. If the pesto is too thick, add a little more water or olive oil until you reach your desired consistency.

6. Transfer the pesto to an airtight container.

Jazz's Tricks

- Homemade pesto can be stored in the refrigerator for up to 1 week. To prevent discoloration, lightly drizzle the surface with extra olive oil before sealing the container.
- Pesto freezes well. To freeze, spoon it into an ice cube tray or small containers and freeze. Once frozen, transfer to a freezer bag or airtight container and store for up to 3 months. Thaw in the refrigerator before using.
- Feel free to substitute walnuts with pine nuts or almonds for a different flavor profile.

COPYCAT CHICK-FIL-A HOMEMADE AVOCADO RANCH SALAD DRESSING

Yield: about 1 ½ cups | Total time: 5 Min

I love the Chick-fil-A avocado ranch but when I look at the ingredient list, it honestly scares me. That's why I made my own version, tastes similar but it's made with healthy fats and no ingredients that will harm your health! We love adding this to sandwiches too!

INGREDIENTS

- 1 large avocado, seed and skin removed
- 1/2 cup plain Greek yogurt
- 1 tablespoon lemon juice
- 1/2 teaspoon dried parsley
- 1/2 teaspoon dried dill
- 1/2 teaspoon dried chives
- 1/2 teaspoon onion powder
- 1/4 teaspoon garlic powder
- 1/4 teaspoon salt
- Black pepper to taste
- Optional: Water (to achieve desired consistency)

INSTRUCTIONS

1. Add all ingredients into a high-speed blender.

CREAMY GARLIC MAYO SAUCE

Yield: about 1 cup | Total Time: 5 Min

INGREDIENTS

- 1 cup mayonnaise
- 3 cloves garlic, minced
- 1 tablespoon lemon juice
- 1/2 teaspoon salt
- 1/4 teaspoon black pepper
- 1/4 teaspoon garlic powder (optional for extra garlic flavor)
- 1 tablespoon olive oil

INSTRUCTIONS

1. In a small bowl, combine the mayonnaise, minced garlic, lemon juice, salt, and black pepper.
2. Whisk in the olive oil until the mixture is smooth and creamy.
3. Taste and adjust seasoning if needed. For a stronger garlic flavor, you can add the optional garlic powder.
4. Cover and refrigerate for at least 30 minutes to let the flavors meld together.

Snacks and Dessert

Sweet treats with a healthier twist

I've always had a sweet tooth, so I'm excited to share these better-for-you desserts. From rich cookies to protein-packed snacks, these recipes let you indulge while keeping things a little more nutritious. I hope you enjoy them as much as I do!

CHOCOLATE ALMOND BUTTER COOKIES

Yield: 12 cookies | Total Time: 25 Min

INGREDIENTS

Wet Ingredients

- 2 ripe bananas, mashed
- 1/3 cup plant-based milk
- 3 tablespoons almond butter
- 1/2 teaspoon vanilla

Dry Ingredients

- 1 cup almond flour
- 1 tablespoon cacao powder
- 1 teaspoon baking powder
- 1/3 cup chocolate chips

When I was plant-based, I used to make this recipe weekly! It was my go-to for a sweet treat after dinner. It's crazy how easy it is!

INSTRUCTIONS

1. Preheat the oven to 350 degrees Fahrenheit.
2. Combine the wet ingredients in a medium bowl. Add the dry ingredients to a separate small bowl.
3. Add the dry ingredients to the bowl with the wet ingredients and mix well with a rubber spatula. Then, stir in the chocolate chips carefully.
4. Scoop cookies onto a parchment paper-lined baking sheet.
5. Bake at 350 degrees Fahrenheit for 18-22 mins.
6. Finish with a melted chocolate drizzle, if desired (melt chocolate chips with a bit of coconut oil). Let the cookies sit for about 15 minutes before digging in.

HIGH-PROTEIN BANANA BREAD MUFFINS (OIL-FREE)

Yield:12 Muffins | Total Time: 40 Min

INGREDIENTS

Wet Ingredients

- 1 cup mashed banana (about 3 large bananas)
- 1 egg
- 2/3 cup brown sugar
- 1/4 cup applesauce

Dry Ingredients

- 3/4 cup oat flour (use gluten-free if necessary)
- 1/2 cup protein powder (I used an unflavored, no-sugar one but use what you have on hand)
- 1 teaspoon baking powder
- 1 teaspoon baking soda
- 1 teaspoon cinnamon
- 1/2 teaspoon ground ginger
- 1 cup chopped walnuts

I felt like all banana bread recipes were packed with sugar and carbohydrates. I wanted something that felt more wholesome, like you could have it for breakfast alongside some Greek yogurt. I make these every single time I have brown bananas!

INSTRUCTIONS

1. Preheat the oven to 350F.
2. While the oven is preheating, add your walnuts to a baking sheet and throw them in the oven for about 10 minutes to toast up. This will add so much flavor into your banana bread muffins. After 10 minutes, remove them from the oven and let them sit on the counter until you're ready to add them in.
3. Peel your ripe bananas and add them to a large bowl. Mash them with a fork until relatively smooth.
4. To the same bowl, add your egg, brown sugar and applesauce! Mix to combine with that same fork.
5. In a separate bowl, add oat flour, protein powder, baking powder, baking soda, cinnamon and ginger. You can even put this through a sieve if you want it to be nice and smooth. I usually do that with all of the ingredients besides the oat flour since I make that myself.
6. Add the dry ingredients into the wet ingredients and mix a few times with a wooden spoon until combined, try not to overmix the batter.
7. Sprinkle in the toasted walnuts and fold the batter.
8. Line a muffin tin with 12 muffin liners, spray with a little oil (just so it doesn't stick).
9. Use an ice cream scooper to get even scoops into the muffin tins, careful not to fill them up all the way. I usually go with 3/4 cup full.
10. Bake the muffins at 350F for about 20-22 minutes. Every oven is different so you just want to make sure you check them at 20 minutes.
11. Put a toothpick into the center of a muffin closest to the back of the oven and closest to the door. If it comes out clean, it's good to pull out! Let them cool for 10-15 minutes. If the one at the front of the oven is not yet done, rotate the pan!

Jazz's Tricks

Storage/Serving Instructions:

1. I like to store mine in a jar in the fridge for maximum freshness! They will last for about 5 days in the fridge.
2. You can also freeze them for 2 months! If you do freeze them, just freeze on a sheet pan in a single layer until they are frozen. Then transfer into a plastic bag (this will just help them from not sticking together).
3. These are delicious warmed up for 1 minute in the air fryer or 15 seconds in the microwave.
4. Enjoy them as an on-the-go breakfast, an easy snack or even dessert!
5. Add peanut butter on top for extra flavor!

VEGAN COCONUT WHIPPED CREAM

Servings: 1 cup | Total time: 5 minutes (plus chilling overnight)

INGREDIENTS

- 1 can of full-fat canned coconut cream
- 1 teaspoon vanilla extract
- 2 tablespoons maple syrup

This is so good on fruit, puddings, ice cream or cake!

INSTRUCTIONS

1. Place the canned coconut cream in the refrigerator overnight. Tip: When selecting a can at the store, avoid shaking it to keep the cream and water separated, which is essential for proper consistency.

2. After refrigerating, carefully open the can without shaking it. Use a spoon to scoop out the solidified coconut cream on top and transfer it to a mixing bowl. Note: If the cream hasn't hardened, it may be due to a bad can.

3. Using a hand mixer, whip the coconut cream until smooth, about 45 seconds.

4. Add the vanilla extract and maple syrup to the whipped coconut cream. Whip again for an additional 15 seconds until everything is well combined.

5. Taste the whipped cream to see if it needs additional sweetener or flavor. Feel free to add more maple syrup or vanilla if desired.

Storage: Store any leftovers in an airtight container in the refrigerator for up to 3-4 days. If it hardens, simply re-whip before serving.

AIR FRYER APPLES

Yield: 1-2 Servings | Total Time: 14 Min

INGREDIENTS

- 2 apples, cut into cubes
- 2 tablespoons of maple syrup
- 2 teaspoons coconut oil, melted
- 1 teaspoon ground cinnamon
- ⅛ teaspoon of ground ginger

INSTRUCTIONS

1. Begin by washing then dicing your apples into even cubes.
2. Add the apples to a bowl along with the liquid sweetener, coconut oil, cinnamon and ginger.
3. Mix well with a spoon to coat the apples.
4. Place in the air fryer at 390F for about 12 minutes, shaking them half way through.
5. Remove from the air fryer and serve with yogurt, vanilla ice cream or coconut whipped cream (see page 196)

Air Fryer Apples were my dessert every night when I was eating a sugar-free diet. I loved how sweet they were and, with the creamy coconut whipped cream on top, it was such a perfect fall dessert. Sometimes, I would even add them to the top of my oatmeal bowls!

AIR FRYER DONUT HOLES

Prep Time: 12 Min | Total Time: 28 Min

I created these easy donut holes when I was craving donuts one day. But I didn't want to add yeast, wait for them to rise and all that jazz. They are so fluffy packed with protein and, every time I make it, I honestly have to try to not eat the whole batch at once.

INGREDIENTS

Donut Holes

- 1 cup gluten-free all-purpose flour
- 1 1/2 teaspoon baking powder
- 1/2 teaspoon salt
- 3/4 cup plain Greek yogurt
- 1 teaspoon vanilla
- Avocado or olive oil spray

Glaze:

- 2 teaspoons of milk
- 2-3 teaspoons of powdered sugar or monk fruit

INSTRUCTIONS

1. Pour the flour, baking powder and salt through a sieve to remove all of the clumps. Place that flour in a large bowl.

2. Add the thick Greek yogurt and vanilla to the flour and knead until it forms into a dough. This may get a bit messy. But just keep kneading until a dough ball forms. You may need to add 1 teaspoon of flour or Greek yogurt depending on the consistency. Every flour and yogurt is different.

3. Divide the dough into 16 equal parts, about golf ball sizes. It helps to do this on a floured surface so it does not stick to the surface and rolls easily.

4. Place the dough balls into the air fryer in a single layer. Spray with some avocado oil or olive oil spray. Toss to coat.

5. Air fry at 350F for 9 minutes, giving them a slight toss halfway through.

6. While the dough balls are in the air fryer, mix together the milk and powered sugar to create a smooth glaze.

7. Let the donut holes cool, then dip into the glaze. Allow the glaze to harden.

8. Enjoy!

FRUIT SALAD RECIPE

Yield: 8 Servings | Total Time: 15 Min

I grew up eating fruit as dessert in my house every night. It really is the best dessert. The simple sauce I made to put on top of this brings it all together. I often make this in the fall for our 40-person Thanksgiving feast for dessert! Everyone loves it.

INGREDIENTS

- 1 cup red grapes
- 2 apples
- 2 oranges
- 2 pears
- 1/4 cup chopped walnuts (optional, for added crunch)
- 2 tablespoons honey
- 2 tablespoons freshly-squeezed orange juice
- 1 teaspoon orange zest
- 1 teaspoon pumpkin pie spice
- Fresh mint leaves for garnish

INSTRUCTIONS

Prepare the Fruit

1. Wash the grapes thoroughly and cut them in half.
2. Wash, core and dice the apples. You can leave the skin on for added color and texture.
3. Peel the oranges and separate them into segments, removing any seeds or pith.
4. Wash, core and dice the pears. Leave the skin on for extra texture.

Dressing

1. In a small bowl, whisk together the honey, orange juice, and pumpkin pie spice. Adjust the amount of honey and pumpkin pie spice to suit your taste preferences. You can add a bit more honey for extra sweetness or pumpkin pie spice for a warm, autumnal flavor.

Assembly

1. In a large mixing bowl, combine the red grapes, diced apples, orange segments, and diced pears. Gently toss them together to distribute the flavors.
2. Add the walnuts for an added crunch.
3. Drizzle the honey-pumpkin pie spice dressing over the fruit in the large mixing bowl.
4. Gently toss the fruit salad, ensuring that all the fruits are coated with the sweet and spiced dressing. Be careful not to mash the fruits; you want to keep them intact.
5. If time allows, cover the bowl with a wrap and chill in the refrigerator for 30 minutes.

NO-BAKE COOKIE DOUGH BLISS BALLS

Yield: 12-19 Balls | Total Time: 10 Min

No-Bake Cookie Dough Bliss Balls are the perfect meal-prepped snack for your week ahead! Make them with your kids & store them in the fridge for a little treat!

INGREDIENTS

- 1 1/2 cups rolled oats
- 1/3 cup protein (any flavor you like)
- 3 tablespoons maple syrup or honey
- 1/2 teaspoon cinnamon
- 1/2 teaspoon salt
- 1/2 cup nut or seed butter
- 1 teaspoon vanilla
- 1/3 cup dairy-free chocolate chips
- 1/3 cup plant-based milk + more or less depending on how the batter comes together.

INSTRUCTIONS

1. Add all of the ingredients to a food processor, blender, or a large bowl. Using a food processor or blender will be a bit easier to mix, but may create less of a bite/chew in the cookie dough balls.
2. Mix for 30 seconds until a sticky mixture forms.
3. Roll into balls & pop these in the fridge to set for 30 minutes!

EASY NO-BAKE PROTEIN BARS

Yield: 8 Bars | Total Time: 1 Hour & 10 Minutes

These protein-packed snacks are naturally sweetened and made with just a few simple, healthy ingredients like creamy peanut butter, agave, chocolate, coconut oil, and plant-based protein powder.

INGREDIENTS

Protein Base:

- 1 cup peanut butter or any nut butter
- 2/3 cup protein powder
- 1/4 cup agave
- 1 teaspoon vanilla extract
- 1/2 teaspoon salt

Chocolate Coating:

- 2 oz chocolate bar (dark or semi-sweet)
- 1/2 teaspoon coconut oil

INSTRUCTIONS

1. To create the protein base, in a large mixing bowl, combine the nut butter, protein powder, agave, vanilla and salt. Stir it together until a thick, dough-like consistency is formed. If the mixture is too dry, you can add a bit more nut butter or a splash of water to achieve the desired texture.

2. Line a loaf pan with parchment paper. Press the protein mixture evenly into the bottom of the pan to form a solid base.

3. To melt the chocolate, chop the chocolate bar into smaller pieces and add it into a microwave-safe bowl. Add the coconut oil to the chocolate. Microwave the chocolate in 30-second increments, stirring well after each interval, until the chocolate is completely melted and smooth.

4. Pour the smooth melted chocolate on top of the protein base, and spread it evenly to coat the entire surface.

5. Place the loaf pan into the freezer to chill and set for 60 minutes until the bars are firm.

6. Once set, remove from the loaf pan and place it onto a cutting board, slice into 8 equal slices.

7. Store the protein bars in an airtight container in the fridge or freezer! The fridge will yield a softer texture and the freezer will yield a more firm texture.

CHOCOLATE CHEESECAKE PUDDING

Yield: 2 Servings | Total Time: 40 Min

INGREDIENTS

- 1 1/4 cups cottage cheese
- 1/4 cup maple syrup
- 2 tablespoons cacao powder
- 2 tablespoons chia seeds
- 1/2 teaspoon vanilla extract
- 1 tablespoon chocolate chips (optional, for topping)
- 1 tablespoon whipped cream (optional, for topping)

INSTRUCTIONS

1. In a food processor, blender, or large bowl, combine the cottage cheese, maple syrup, cacao powder, chia seeds, and vanilla extract.
2. Blend until smooth. If you're using a bowl, you'll need an immersion blender for this.
3. Transfer the smooth mixture into a jar or small container.
4. Cover and refrigerate for 30 minutes, allowing the pudding to thicken.
5. Before serving, top with chocolate chips and whipped cream, if desired.

BROWN BUTTER CHOCOLATE CHIP COOKIES

Yield: 12 Cookies | Total Time: 2 Hrs

INGREDIENTS

Wet Ingredients

- 3/4 cup unsalted butter, about 1 1/2 sticks
- 1 cup coconut sugar
- 1 large egg
- 1 large egg yolk
- 1 tablespoon vanilla extract

Dry ingredients

- 1 3/4 cups gluten-free baking flour
- 3/4 teaspoon baking soda
- 1 teaspoon salt
- 1 1/2 cups chocolate chips

INSTRUCTIONS

1. Cut the butter into small cubes and place them in a saucepan over medium heat.

2. Stir constantly for about 7-9 minutes until the butter foams, turns brown, and has a nutty aroma.

3. Remove from heat and pour into a bowl. Cool in the fridge for 20 minutes. Ensure the brown butter is cool before mixing with the other ingredients to avoid melting the sugar and creating a runny dough.

4. Once the brown butter is cooled, mix the wet ingredients in a large bowl or stand mixer. Add the cooled brown butter, coconut sugar, egg, egg yolk, and vanilla extract. Beat until well combined.

5. In a separate bowl, sift together the dry ingredients—gluten-free flour, baking soda, and salt—to remove any clumps.

6. Gradually add the dry ingredients to the wet mixture, about 1/4 cup at a time, mixing gently each time. Do not overmix.

7. Gently fold in the chocolate chips.

8. Cover the bowl and refrigerate the dough for at least 30 minutes, or up to 12 hours.

9. Preheat the oven to 350°F (175°C).

10. Scoop the dough onto a lined cookie sheet, spacing each scoop about 2 inches apart.

11. Bake for 11 minutes, until the edges are golden and the centers are chewy.

12. Let the cookies cool on the baking sheet for a few minutes before transferring them to a wire rack to cool completely.

COPYCAT SAMOAS COOKIES

Yield: 12 Cookies | Preparation Time: 20 Min

INGREDIENTS

- 1 cup pitted Medjool dates
- 2 cups hot water
- 1 cup shredded coconut
- 1 teaspoon vanilla extract
- 1/3 cup cacao powder
- 2 tablespoons coconut oil, melted and warm
- 2 tablespoons maple syrup

INSTRUCTIONS

1. Soak the pitted Medjool dates in hot water for 5 minutes.

2. While the dates are soaking, toast the shredded coconut in a skillet over medium heat for about 5 minutes, until golden brown, stirring occasionally.

3. Drain the dates and add them to a food processor along with the toasted coconut and vanilla extract. Pulse until the mixture becomes sticky and well combined.

4. Roll the mixture into 12 even balls and flatten each one with your fingers to form cookie shapes. Place the cookies on a parchment paper lined baking sheet and freeze for 10 minutes.

5. While the cookies are in the freezer, prepare the chocolate coating by mixing cacao powder, melted coconut oil, and maple syrup in a bowl until smooth.

6. Remove the cookies from the freezer. Dip the bottom of each cookie in the chocolate mixture, then drizzle the remaining chocolate over the top of the cookies.

7. Return the cookies to the parchment paper lined baking sheet and freeze for another 10 minutes to set the chocolate.

Jazz's Tricks

- If your dates are a bit dry, soak them for an additional 2-3 minutes to ensure they blend smoothly.
- Keep a close eye on the coconut while toasting; it can go from golden to burnt quickly.
- If the chocolate mixture becomes too thick, gently reheat it or add a bit more melted coconut oil.

SALTED CARAMEL SAUCE

Yield: ¾ cup | Preparation Time: 15 Min

Whether drizzled over fruit, swirled into oatmeal, or added to lattes or yogurt bowls, this sauce is versatile! Not only that, it's dairy-free, making it suitable for a range of diets.

INGREDIENTS

- 1/2 cup canned coconut milk (full-fat)
- 1/4 cup coconut sugar
- 2 tablespoons peanut butter
- 1/2 teaspoon vanilla extract
- 1/2 teaspoon pink salt

INSTRUCTIONS

1. In a small saucepan, combine the coconut milk and coconut sugar. Stir over medium heat until the sugar dissolves.

2. Bring the mixture to a gentle simmer, stirring constantly. Continue to cook for about 5-7 minutes, or until the sauce thickens and becomes smooth.

3. Remove from heat and stir in the almond butter, vanilla extract, and a pinch of sea salt. Mix well until fully combined and smooth.

4. Let the caramel cool slightly; it will thicken as it cools. Drizzle over your favorite desserts, fruits, or breakfast dishes.

DUTCH APPLE PIE

Yield: 6-8 | Preparation Time: 50 Min

Nothing beats the smell of a freshly baked homemade apple pie, but sometimes I'm just not in the mood to roll out the dough that a traditional apple pie requires. My version is incredibly easy to make, plus it's refined-sugar-free and vegan!

INGREDIENTS

For the Apples:

- 1 pre-made pie crust (thawed for 10 minutes)
- 4 Granny Smith apples (or any tart apple), diced
- 2 tablespoons water or apple juice
- 2 tablespoons lemon juice
- 1 teaspoon vanilla extract
- 1 teaspoon cinnamon
- 1/2 teaspoon nutmeg

For the Crumble Topping:

- 3/4 cup rolled oats
- 1/2 cup almond flour
- 1/2 cup coconut sugar
- 1/2 cup chopped walnuts or pecans
- 1/4 cup melted coconut oil
- 1/4 teaspoon cinnamon
- Pinch of salt

INSTRUCTIONS

1. Preheat your oven to 350°F (175°C). Take the thawed pie crust and set it aside for filling.

2. In a large mixing bowl, combine the diced apples, water (or apple juice), lemon juice, vanilla extract, cinnamon, and nutmeg. Stir until the apples are well-coated with the mixture.

3. Transfer the apple mixture into the prepared pie crust, spreading it evenly. Place the pie in the oven and bake for 10 minutes.

4. While the apple filling bakes, prepare the crumble topping. In another bowl, mix together the oats, almond flour, chopped nuts, melted coconut oil, cinnamon, and a pinch of salt. Stir until everything is well combined and has a crumbly texture.

5. After 10 minutes, carefully remove the pie from the oven. Evenly sprinkle the crumble topping over the partially baked apples.

6. Return the pie to the oven and bake for an additional 40 minutes, or until the topping is golden and the apples are soft.

7. Serve the pie warm, either on its own or with a dollop of Greek yogurt, vanilla ice cream, or dairy-free coconut yogurt if desired. Enjoy!

Grocery Shopping Made Simple

A note from the author:

Grocery lists are a great place to start when you're looking to eat healthy meals at home. I know how overwhelming it can feel walking into a grocery store, not sure where to begin or what ingredients to buy. That's why I've put together this simple guide to help you stock up on what's readily available at your local grocery store, so you're always prepared to make the recipes in this book.

Not every ingredient listed in the recipes in this book is on this grocery list, but this is a fantastic place to start. My goal is to make grocery shopping less stressful and set you up for success in your kitchen. My experience shows that building a pantry and fridge with healthy essentials can make cooking meals easier and much less stressful.

To make the most of your budget, I recommend checking out the weekly sales at your favorite grocery stores. I often look for buy-one-get-one-free deals or discounts on pantry staples. Stocking up during sales is a great way to save money while keeping your kitchen full of essentials for healthy meals.

With this list and these tips in hand, you'll be ready to confidently navigate the grocery aisles and start cooking up delicious, wholesome meals at home!

A NOTE ON ORGANIC VS. NON ORGANIC

Whenever possible, I like to buy organic and non-GMO products to avoid unnecessary chemicals. Here's a list of the foods to buy organic if you can. It is often referred to as the **Dirty Dozen**. These foods tend to have the highest pesticide residues, so going organic is a healthier choice when purchasing them:

Dirty Dozen

1. Strawberries
2. Spinach
3. Kale, Collard & Mustard Greens
4. Peaches
5. Pears
6. Nectarines
7. Apples
8. Grapes
9. Bell Peppers & Hot Peppers
10. Cherries
11. Blueberries
12. Green Beans

Additional Items to Consider Buying Organic:

- Tomatoes
- Celery
- Cucumbers
- Potatoes
- Carrots

These items tend to absorb more pesticides due to their thin skin or because they're grown with a lot of chemicals. Going organic with these will help reduce your exposure.

For other produce with thicker skin, like avocados, pineapples, or bananas, you don't need to prioritize organic as much. However, it's always good to aim for organic when you can!

A NOTE ON INFLAMMATORY OILS

When purchasing pre-packaged items like frozen veggies, hummus, pesto, or pasta sauce, always check the ingredient label on the back. Make sure the product is free from **inflammatory oils like canola oil, soybean oil, cottonseed oil, sunflower oil, or corn oil**. These oils are often hidden in processed foods and can negatively impact your health. Look for items made with healthier options like olive oil or avocado oil.

A NOTE ON SUGAR

Similarly, watch out for added sugars sneaking into your food. Common names for added sugars include **high-fructose corn syrup, dextrose, sucrose, maltose, and even "evaporated cane juice."** You'd be surprised how many products contain hidden sugars! Take a look at your breads, a common spot sugar can hide!

Here's a list of the groceries I try to keep on hand:

Produce:

- Apples (green & red)
- Avocados
- Bananas
- Bell Peppers
- Broccoli
- Carrots
- Celery
- Cucumbers
- Kale
- Spinach
- Fresh Ginger
- Sweet Potatoes
- Tomatoes
- Zucchini
- Lemons
- Limes
- Strawberries
- Pears
- Red & Yellow Onions

Proteins:

- Organic Chicken (fresh/frozen)
- Pasture-Raised Beef
- Wild Atlantic Salmon (fresh/frozen)
- Wild-caught shrimp (look for shrimp from U.S. waters)
- Organic/Pasture-Raised Eggs

Dairy/Refrigerated:

- Plain Greek Yogurt (full-fat or dairy-free)
- Feta Cheese (or dairy-free feta)
- Hummus
- Pesto (or dairy-free pesto)
- Almond Milk (or other plant-based milk)
- Oat milk
- Canned Coconut Milk

Oils/Vinegars/Sauces:

- Extra Virgin Olive Oil
- Avocado Oil
- Coconut Oil
- Balsamic Vinegar
- Red Wine Vinegar
- Apple Cider Vinegar
- Dijon Mustard
- Salsa
- Tahini

Spices/Seasonings:

- Pink Himalayan Salt
- Black Pepper
- Garlic Powder
- Onion Powder
- Paprika
- Dried Basil
- Dried Oregano
- Dried Parsley
- Cinnamon
- Turmeric Powder
- Nutmeg
- Curry Powder
- Nutritional Yeast
- Sesame Seeds
- Everything Bagel Seasoning
- Pumpkin Pie Spice
- Saffron
- Sumac

Nuts & Seeds:

- Raw, unroasted, and unsalted Almonds
- Raw, unroasted, and unsalted Cashews
- Raw, unroasted, and unsalted Pecans
- Raw, unroasted, and unsalted Walnuts
- Chia Seeds
- Hemp Seeds
- Ground Flaxseeds
- Almond Butter (look for no added oils, sugar, or salt)
- Peanut Butter (look for no added oils, sugar, or salt)
- Pumpkin Seeds (look for no added oils, sugar, or salt)
- Sunflower Seed Butter(great for a nut-free alternative)

Grains/Legumes:

- Quinoa
- Basmati rice
- Brown Rice
- Canned Chickpeas
- Canned Kidney Beans
- Canned Black Beans
- Gluten-free pasta made from brown rice
- Organic gluten-free oats, quick cooking or whole

Frozen:

- Frozen Blueberries
- Frozen Broccoli
- Frozen Cauliflower
- Frozen Riced Cauliflower
- Green Peas

Beverages:

- Green Tea
- Matcha Green Tea Powder
- Chamomile Tea
- Peppermint Tea
- Ginger Tea

Supplements:

- Chocolate Protein Powder
- Vanilla Protein Powder
- Collagen

Pantry:

- Gluten-free Flour
- Almond Flour
- Coconut Flour
- Baking Powder
- Baking Soda
- Coconut Sugar
- Cacao Powder
- 100% Pure Maple Syrup
- Raw Honey
- Dates
- Raisins
- Black Olives
- Kalamata Olives
- Chicken Broth or Vegetable Broth (Stock can also be used)

The Importance of Protein, Carbs, and Fats

Our bodies need three main macronutrients to function properly: protein, carbohydrates, and fats. These nutrients serve different purposes and are essential to your overall health, so it's important to understand why they're necessary and how to choose the best sources!

Protein

Protein is like the building block for your body. It helps repair muscles, supports your immune system, and is vital for healthy hair, skin, and nails. When you eat protein, it breaks down into amino acids, which your body uses to build and repair tissues. This is especially important if you exercise or want to maintain a healthy metabolism. It's great to aim for half your body weight daily, in grams. An example: if you weigh 160 lbs, to aim for 80g protein daily.

Good sources of protein include lean meats like chicken or turkey, fish, eggs, tofu, beans, and lentils. Less ideal sources might be highly processed meats, like hot dogs or deli meats, which often contain added sodium and preservatives.

Carbohydrates

Carbs provide your body with energy. They turn into sugar in your bloodstream, giving you the fuel you need to stay active throughout the day.

The best kind of carbs come from whole foods like fruits, vegetables, and whole grains, which also give you fiber to keep your digestive system healthy. Processed carbs, like white bread, sugary cereals, and sweets, can cause spikes in blood sugar and don't provide lasting energy. It's best to focus on complex carbs like brown rice, quinoa, and oats, which digest more slowly and keep you full longer.

Fats

Fats are necessary for hormone production, brain function, and absorbing important vitamins (A, D, E, and K). They also give you a longer-lasting source of energy and keep you fuller for longer.

Healthy fats come from foods like avocados, nuts, seeds, olive oil, and fatty fish like salmon. These fats can help lower bad cholesterol and support heart health. On the other hand, trans fats and too many saturated fats found in fried foods, baked goods, and processed snacks can lead to health issues like heart disease over time. Choose fats wisely to fuel your body properly.

Why it's important!

When I create recipes, I keep the balance of protein, carbs, and fats in mind. My goal is to ensure that every meal not only tastes great but also fuels your body in the best way possible. Each ingredient is thoughtfully selected to provide the right mix of these macronutrients so you can feel satisfied, energized, and nourished! Happy cooking, friend!